MARTIAL ARTS of the ORIENT

Peter Lewis

GALLERY BOOKS
An Imprint of W. H. Smith Publishers Inc.
112 Madison Avenue
New York City 10016

DEDICATION
*For Joe Johal,
a true martial artist and a brother.*

This book was devised and produced by
Multimedia Publications (UK) Ltd

Editor: Jeff Groman
Production: Arnon Orbach
Design: Terry Allen
Picture Research: Vivien Fraser

First published in the United States of America 1985
by Gallery Books, an imprint of W. H. Smith
Publishers Inc., 112 Madison Avenue, New York,
NY 10016.
Reprinted 1986

ISBN 0 8317 5804 X

Typeset by Keene Graphics Ltd, London
Origination by Imago
Printed in Italy by Sagdos

CONTENTS

Introduction

Fighting is as old as man himself. This struggle to overcome another by means of combat, unarmed or armed, is perhaps the legacy handed down to us from our ancestors, the cave dwellers. Man has formulated scientific principles through the ages in his efforts to subdue enemies by fair means or foul. This quest for domination sowed the seeds for a fighting art.

The term 'martial arts' simply means arts concerned with the waging of war. Many of the martial arts we know today were developed from ancient war skills. In time, man's search for a deeper meaning to life, led to the development of a higher level of fighting. Ultimately, the old martial ways were used to cultivate man's understanding of himself.

This paradox of beginning a lethal skill and along the way transcending the violent aims of that skill to become a human being with superior qualities in both mind and body, is perhaps best summed up by the Chinese proverb, 'He who overcomes others is strong. He who overcomes himself is mighty'.

The martial arts of the Orient are shrouded in mystery and tradition. Each country seems to have developed its own fighting skills and through trial and error, honed them to perfection. Although many of these fighting arts differ tremendously from one another, there is one constant throughout — that is the almost pathological urge for anonymity. It is because of this brotherhood of secrecy that many of the martial arts we know today have only come to light within the last 50 years or so.

Many martial arts of the East have their roots buried deeply in religion. *Taoism* and *Buddhism* and their many offshoots have all played important roles in the development of fighting systems. The servants of these religious disciplines, the monks and priests, were for the most part responsible for spreading the various fighting skills all over Asia.

The spread of martial arts in the United States was largely because of the Korean War and not, as most people think, because of World War Two. At that time, all martial arts were banned in Japan on orders from General McArthur. During the Korean War, many US servicemen stationed in Seoul and Tokyo had their first confrontation with the so-called 'martial arts'. This nucleus of returning servicemen brought their new fighting skills with them, and thus initiated martial arts in America. Other contributory influences in the late 1960s and early 1970s were kung fu movies and the growing violence on the streets. Thus a new era for these age-old fighting skills of the Orient had begun.

6

Karate

*A gem is not polished without rubbing
nor a man perfected without trials.*

Previous pages *A kung fu adept adopts a praying mantis pose. His hands position resembles that of the mantis' claw.*

Left *Young karate blackbelts kneel in meditation before the daily practice session begins. The polished wooden floor is typical of a Japanese dojo.*

Right *A gojo-ryu karate stylist executing a traditional knife hand block. This karate style comes from Okinawa and its practitioners use a mixture of hard and soft techniques.*

Meaning and Early Origins

Karate literally means 'empty hand', although the correct term is *karate-do,* or 'way of the empty hand'. Karate comes from Okinawa, one of the Ryukyu Islands that form a chain of stepping stones between Japan and China. Because of their geographical position, it was there that the cultures of Japan and China met and fermented. In 1609, the island of Okinawa was invaded by Japanese troops. To prevent insurrection, the ruler of the island was taken back to Japan as a hostage and the Japanese quickly set up a police force in the capital, Naha. This was to superintend internal affairs. Their next step was to ban the military class and confiscate all arms. The Japanese were confident that, without weapons, the Ryukyu islanders could not rebel.

But the invaders had reckoned without the ancestral heritage of this island race — that of their martial arts. Because of Okinawa's close trade ties with China. The kung fu styles and methods of the latter country had mixed with the islanders' indigenous fighting arts.

Those unarmed arts were known as Okinawa *T'ang* or *Te,* which means 'hand'. Next, the Ryukyu islanders, after consulting the old monks in the mountains, began to toughen their knuckles and elbows on straw pads and wet sand. Graduating to tree trunks, they pounded their fists into the trees day after day until eventually huge callouses built up on various parts of their bodies.

Fighting Back

The armor of Japanese troops and even of the Samurai, was made from lacquered bamboo and leather thongs. So when the Okinawans decided the time had come to fight back in guerilla attacks, their deadly hardened fingers easily penetrated the armor of their oppressors, killing them instantly. When the Japanese sent mounted troops to quell the outbreaks of rebellion, the islanders devised a series of lethal kicks, executed while flying through the air. So even a mounted enemy proved to be no obstacle. The farmers played their part in fighting back by transforming

agricultural implements into deadly weapons. The handle of a rice grinder, called a *tonfa,* was used to parry the blows from a Samurai sword. The sickle for cutting the crops, known as *kama,* made an excellent weapon against spear and sword attacks.

It was the transformation of these farming implements that today has given rise in the martial arts to Okinawan kobudo — the study of the classical weaponry of Okinawa.

The Birth of Modern Karate
Gradually, the Okinawans grew resigned to the fact that their Japanese overlords were going to stay forever. So they accepted the occupation with distaste but allegiance. In 1868 a man was born named Gichin Funakoshi, the son of a minor official on Okinawa. The young Funakoshi grew up learning the martial skills of Okinawan Te from a great master named Azato. By the time he was 25, Gichin Funakoshi had mastered the art and had also become a school teacher. When a visiting schools commissioner witnessed a demonstration of his art, Gichin Funakoshi was authorized to put martial arts on the educational curriculum. Karate had at last come out into the open, and was to be taught in schools throughout Okinawa.

First Demonstration
Japan's introduction to what is now known as karate had to wait until 1912. It was then that the Imperial Navy's fleet, under Admiral Dewa, anchored in Chujo Bay, Okinawa. The ships' crews were housed in the school were Gichin Funakoshi taught, and the schoolmaster often put on impromptu demonstrations of karate for them. It was through this that karate came to be talked about in Tokyo. Nearly 10 years later, in 1921, the Emperor of Japan asked Funakoshi to perform his art in front of him. So impressed

was the emperor at this exhibition of fighting skill, that he asked Funakoshi to travel to Japan and teach his art there. Within five years the mild-mannered Okinawan school teacher had become the idol of Japanese martial arts circles. By now Gichin Funakoshi was approaching his 60th birthday. He set up his first training school, or 'dojo', in Tokyo. It was known as *Shotokan,* or the 'club of Shoto'. Funakoshi had previously used the pen-name of Shoto when he used to write poetry, so he felt that this name was quite appropriate. *Shoto* means 'waving pines'. Gichin Funakoshi had laid down the foundation for the biggest school of karate in the world. Although at that time his art was still known as Okinawan hand, it was later changed into Japanese calligraphy to read *karate-do,* or 'the way of the empty hand'.

Major Schools and Styles of Karate
The influence of Funakoshi's new karate caused a rapid increase of karate schools in Japan as other masters from Okinawa went over to teach their own particular styles. Hot on the heels of Funakoshi was Chojun Miyagi of the Gojuryu school, and Kenwa Mabuni of the Shitoryu school. Many others came after them and pioneered the development of wadoryu, shotokai, kyokushinkai, and shukokai. Today millions of karate practitioners all over the world practice any one of 15 major styles and their offshoots, which have come out of Japan.

In America, the first properly organized karate association was started in Los Angeles in 1955. It was begun by a Japanese *sensei* (teacher) named Oshima, trained in the style known as shotokai. In addition to this, several Americans founded their own systems based on karate, which means that karate has only been in America for a little more than 30 years.

Previous pages *A Shotokan karate master blocks a punch to the body and retaliates with a strong backfist strike to the carotid artery. To add more power into this technique, the master emits the super shout of karate known as a* kiai.

Above left *The line-up here represents some of the United States top karate fighters.*

Left and above *In sport karate, where actual bodily strikes are forbidden, the aim is to execute a technique as near as possible to the opponent without actually striking him. Sport karate makes use of sweeping techniques to render an opponent helpless on the floor. A successful move will earn the victor a half or a full point, depending on the referee's assessment of the technique.*

Left *This is a technique from full contact karate. An opponent reacts to a frontal attack, by employing a jumping front kick. The sheer force and power of this kick is enough to stop a man dead in his tracks.*

Right *In some contact karate tournaments novices wear special protective headgear and body armor which is cushioned with padding to prevent injury. Special slip-on padded boots are worn to cut down on injuries received from kicks.* Top: *The fighter is about to employ a front kick.* Bottom: *As the fighter goes in with a roundhouse kick his opponent uses an underarm sweep to stop the kick and retaliates with a hammer fist strike to the head.*

Exciting Spectator Sport

Karate, no longer needed as a killing art against oppressors, has developed into an exciting spectator sport with participants competing at every level for honors. The sport itself is governed by a committee known as the World Union of Karate Organizations which is always in contact with the American Athletic Union. World championships are held every two years, with more than 50 countries taking part. It is hoped that one day karate will become an Olympic sport.

With the development of karate as a major sport, tournaments were held at regular intervals all over America. Non-martial artists went along as spectators, because karate is very visual. But they didn't understand the rules nor how the winner was decided. To make things easier some factions within American karate came up with a system known as Full Contact Karate. This differed from the traditional form of the art, where no body contact is allowed. In the new system, participants wear Western-style boxing gloves and fight in an ordinary boxing ring, but they still retain the punching and kicking techniques of karate. And, as its name denotes, in full contact, contestants actually hit each other.

The idea quickly caught on and this offshoot from karate established itself with a huge following. Television companies soon began to screen contests at peak viewing times and another association, the Professional Karate Association was born, whose emerging champions people could identify with. So popular was this new spectator sport, born in the United States, that it quickly spread around the world. As a result of full contact karate's popularity, the traditionalists revamped their tournaments to include a new section known as sport karate. This is proving to be very successful but it nowhere matches the excitement and fervor generated by a full contact tournament.

What is Karate all about?

Even in early training, the skills of a karate student are lethal because it is an all-in fighting system where everything is allowed. The concept of the art is to use every means available to a practitioner, and to overcome by technique, conditioning, and training an assailant or assailants in his fight for life. This is why karate is based on blows delivered with the hand, foot, head, or knee. When he has mastered all these effective techniques, a student is awarded his first degree black belt, known as *shodan*, and he himself is then regarded as a *sensei*, or teacher.

During training, a strange paradox seems to emerge. Originally, perhaps, the student takes up the art as an effective self-defense system. Then, as a result of hard training and the battles between mind and body in order to achieve instantaneous automatic reaction to any given situation, a feeling of inner calm and peace is experienced. The student reaches the point where he has won the fight within himself, and no longer needs to prove that he can fight. In fact, he will often prefer to walk away from trouble. But should that trouble follow him, he will be more than able to deal with it with deadly efficiency.

Karate Training

The hall or area where a student trains is called the *dojo*. The basic techniques are usually practiced with a partner and then repeated over and over again. The only forbidden act in karate is to injure a training partner or a competition opponent. Ensuring this demands great skill and judgement. Part of the training is also centered on exercises performed against an imaginary opponent. This is called *kata*, and is very similar to shadow boxing. To many traditionalists this is the single most important aspect of karate. Many exponents of the art spend a whole lifetime just perfecting the movements and mental awareness of kata.

The Karate Kiai

A student must become familiar with all the vital areas of the body, and be able to focus a punch or kick on them at any given moment. To aid him during the performance of an impact technique, a *karateka* (one who studies karate) will emit a bloodcurdling shout known as the *kiai*. This kiai is brought up from the very depths of the lungs and emitted through the mouth as a shout, much as a weight-lifter shouts loudly before a heavy lift.

In a way, the kiai does two things. First, it brings a surge of power to a given blow, and second, when confronted with an emergency, this devastating shout from the lips of the intended victim just before he counter-attacks can momentarily confuse the assailant. It will at least put him off guard for those important few seconds before the karateka deals his blow.

Previous pages *In many countries group outdoor karate training sessions are a common sight. The feeling of being next to nature adds to the karate students' spiritual awareness.*

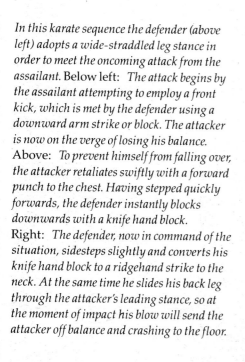

In this karate sequence the defender (above left) adopts a wide-straddled leg stance in order to meet the oncoming attack from the assailant. Below left: The attack begins by the assailant attempting to employ a front kick, which is met by the defender using a downward arm strike or block. The attacker is now on the verge of losing his balance. Above: To prevent himself from falling over, the attacker retaliates swiftly with a forward punch to the chest. Having stepped quickly forwards, the defender instantly blocks downwards with a knife hand block. Right: The defender, now in command of the situation, sidesteps slightly and converts his knife hand block to a ridgehand strike to the neck. At the same time he slides his back leg through the attacker's leading stance, so at the moment of impact his blow will send the attacker off balance and crashing to the floor.

To enable an adept of karate to release the power he has harnessed by learning the art, special tests of power were instituted known as Tamashiwara or power breaking. In employing tamashiwari techniques practitioners have created a whole new field of showbiz, in which different parts of the body are used to break all kinds of materials.

Following pages, **left** *A Japanese instructor demonstrates to the massed ranks of karate students the power of the fist by demolishing a stack of roofing tiles.*

Following pages, right *The flying sidekick. Once the kick is executed and the practitioner is in the air, he has little control — so constant practice is always necessary.*

Tamashiwara

In karate, as in most other martial arts, there is a section called powerbreaking or *tamashiwara.* In this, the student is called upon to break various hard materials by means of a blow from the fist, head, elbow, or even the fingertips. This powerbreaking was originally intended to make the karate student aware of the tremendous power within himself. Today, however, the changing face of the art involves competition between the various martial arts power-breakers to see who can break the most objects or the thickest wood.

The world record for breaking roofing tiles is held by the Japanese master, Masatatsu Oyama, who broke 30 tiles with one blow of his clenched fist.

At karate tournaments throughout America, you will always see at least one demonstration of a tamashiwara expert driving his fist, knife hand (the edge of the hand), elbow, or head through anything from concrete to solid ice. Obviously a high degree of skill and training are necessary before a karateka can attempt such mind-blowing feats.

Mind over Matter

The mind and its powers plays a very important role in the makeup of a good karateka. Many strange stories have emanated from the training halls of Japan over the years. They tell of the great masters performing seemingly impossible feats of endurance, thanks mainly to their finely attuned mental powers. There are stories such as those of feeble old men breaking wood four and five inches thick, with gnarled and withered hands. But there is also the true story of one of karate's greatest heroes, who fought wild bulls with his bare hands. Before he retired he had fought nearly 50 bulls and killed at least three of them with his bare hands.

A well known pioneer of East Coast karate, sensei Peter Urban, tells the story of his master, Richard Kim, who was imprisoned in Manchuria. His captors did not like the way Kim seemed undisturbed by his captivity, so in an effort to make an example of him to the other prisoners they placed Kim in a cage with two tigers. The next morning the Manchurian guards found the tigers dead, with Kim sitting crosslegged in a relaxed pose. The man had no weapons in his possession, so how had he killed the tigers?

Another story tells of the famous gojuryu sensei, Gogen Yamaguchi, whose nickname was The Cat, because he could move so swiftly. He was said to meditate under the full force of a waterfall every morning, and enjoyed the best of health all his life, when other mortals would almost certainly have died of pneumonia.

Scientists have often said that the power of the mind knows no boundaries. This certainly seems to be the case where the martial arts are concerned.

The Karate Dojo

The karate *dojo* is the hall where a karateka practices his art. Upon entering, he must bow from the waist. A great deal of respect and reverence must be shown while training in the dojo. When a student addresses the *sensei* (teacher), he bows before speaking. Strict behavior is enforced and must be adhered to at all times. The students' karate suits are known as *gi*, and must be clean and well pressed. The karate uniform traditionally dates back to that of a simple Japanese peasant's garb. Which was a loose-fitting two-piece affair, with wide baggy trousers.

The suit is held together with a very long belt, usually colored. The color denotes the varying degrees of proficiency of its wearer. An absolute beginner is a white belt. According to the old traditions, when the white belt student passed his first grading exam he was awarded his *kyu* grade — this meant he was entitled to wear a different colored belt. The student would then dye the belt the appropriate color as he progressed through the kyu grades towards his black belt. The colors of the kyu grades become progressively darker with increased proficiency, thus enabling a student to keep the same belt throughout his training, just by dyeing it.

A karate dojo can be centered almost anywhere a sensei wants to teach his art.

Karate Belt Rankings

Regardless of the style and school of karate a practitioner comes from, all students have one goal in mind, and that is to reach the standard of black belt. This can take anything up to five years to achieve. Once attained, the training does not cease; in fact, it becomes even more arduous. The black belt trains in the physical and mental disciplines of the art in an effort to reach the next class of grading. This is called a *Dan*. After his Second Dan, the student will try even harder for his Third Dan, and so on.

This black belt Dan ranking system comes from Japan, where it is used for virtually everything from swimming to *Go* (a board game not unlike checkers).

The highest ranked Japanese black belt is Gogen Yamaguchi, who was ranked at Tenth Dan. Oddly enough, after Ninth Dan the color reverts to red, which is the color of a beginner's belt before he takes his first kyu examination. This symbolizes the fact that when one knows all, he returns to knowing nothing, yet understands everything.

Today, martial arts teachers all over the world have broken away from their traditional teachings and formed their own systems and styles. Because of this they can award themselves any high Dan grade they wish. Therefore it is not uncommon to find teachers with Sixth and Seventh Dan black belts at comparatively young ages.

Above left *A Japanese master of Shotokan karate demonstrating the gyakuzuki or reverse punch. This punch is the most used technique in tournaments and competition today.*

Above center and right
The formal stance in karate is known as naore. The yoi or informal stance is used to begin and end a kata or get ready to fight in competition. The movement is executed by overemphasizing the crossing of the arms and then outstretching them to either side of the body. The finished position is when the body is erect and the fists clenched.

Left *The karate kiai or powershout in execution. The expression on the student's face radiates the sheer force at which the ensuing technique will be delivered.*

Right, above *In the flying sidekick technique, the ridge of the foot of the outstretched leg acts as the weapon. The other leg is kept tucked under protecting the groin from a counter-attack.*

Right, below *Using only his bare hands and feet, a karate master defends himself against multiple attackers.*

Women in the Art

Because of today's constant threat of street violence, including rape, many women are adopting the art of karate as an effective means of protection. Some women go through the full routine in both the traditional and sporting forms of karate. They go on to become fighting superstars on the tournament circuits throughout the country. Many of the old karate techniques have been revamped and styled more towards defense with the female in mind. Every city in every state can boast of at least two or three ladies-only karate clubs, with female instructors ranked Second and Third Dan.

America sends out a full complement of female fighters to the WUKO world championships every time they are staged. Educational chiefs in many states have seen fit to introduce basic karate and karate-type training to mixed groups of children, as early as the sixth grade.

Karate in the Movies

Hollywood was quick to catch on to the popularity of martial arts. From the early 1960s onwards, the fight scenes in films were choreographed to incorporate karate techniques. Television quickly followed the same format and even went a step further and introduced a series called *The Green Hornet* featuring the now legendary Bruce Lee. Since those early days we have seen films such as *Enter The Ninja, The Karate Kid*, as well as Chuck Norris's huge successes both on film and video. Superstars such as James Coburn, Arnold Schwarzenegger, David Carradine, Burt Reynolds, and Elvis Presley all practiced karate.

New stars are now emerging on the movie scene who are martial artists in their own right. The burst of ninja movies has made stars such as Sho Kosugi and ex-contact karate fighter Keith Vitali into household names. Their exploits on the screen are perhaps little short of superhuman.

A woman karate teacher from New York demonstrates a jodan or high area side kick.

Above *Movie and TV star Chuck Norris loosening up before a film stunt. This particular technique is the finish of a flying kick.*

Left *A formidable trio of black belt triplets performing kata in unison.*

The basic kick in karate is the front kick. The body is supported on the front leg which is planted firmly on the ground. The back leg is brought through with tremendous force to deliver the blow. Throughout this technique the fist must constantly guard the face to allow for a counter-attack.

Karate and the Law

In a poll carried out in 26 American cities to discover if the local police departments were familiar with karate and its various techniques, every one of them, with the exception of Pittsburgh, agreed that they were familiar with the art. Although this poll was carried out in 1967, it showed even then that police departments were aware of karate's potential as a law enforcement tool.

Hawaii was the first state to pioneer karate instruction for the guards in its penal institutions, back in the early 1960s. This is not really surprising because the people there are mainly of mixed Asian origin, and most would have been familiar with the various martial systems emanating from the Orient.

A popular belief in the United States is that karate students must register their hands with the police as dangerous weapons. This is a modern myth born out of ignorance. But it is true to say that any felonious assault initiated by a practitioner of karate would be treated by the courts in the same way as someone using a deadly weapon.

By 1981 every law enforcement agency in the United States was believed to be practicing some form of Oriental martial art. Some police departments have even gone a step further and introduced ancient Okinawan weapons to combat crimes of the 20th century.

The Karate Stance

The blows in traditional karate are delivered from a number of stances, each of which is suited to a particular purpose or situation. Certain styles, such as gojuryu, place much emphasis on the stance. When a student has undergone extensive training in stance work, he is put to the test by having planks of wood and long wooden poles broken on his body. Although this does seem to be somewhat masochistic, it does prove to the student what tremendous power he has within himself.

In Japan, a similar test is conducted, but minus the wooden planks. All students who are thought to be ready, line up in the straddle leg stance. The instructor walks up and violently kicks each one of them in the groin. Those that are left standing after this assault on the genitals are deemed worthy of further advanced training.

A form of Korean karate known as kempo. The defender has countered a strike with a sweep to take his man down. He applies a palm heel strike to the face to finish him off.

Kung Fu

*To ask, is a moment's shame, not to ask,
and remain ignorant is a lifelong shame.*

Tao Te Ching

Right *David Carradine, star of the TV series 'Kung Fu', adopts a typical shaolin kung fu position.*

Following pages *Two opponents fighting in a kung fu tournament. Due to the uncontrollable techniques of kung fu, competitions outside of Hong Kong are rarely seen.*

In the previous chapter we saw how karate was exported to Japan from Okinawa, where it grew and developed. There are various theories as to where the martial arts, as we know them today, came from. It is generally accepted that the birthplace of kung fu was in northern China around AD520.

The Wandering Monk

Most of the kung fu practiced today is said to have originated in the Shaolin Monastery on Songshan Mountain, Honan Province, in northern China.

It was introduced there by a wandering Indian monk named Bodhidharma, also known as Ta-Mo. Bodhidharma was the son of King Sugandha of India. As befitted the son of royalty, in his youth Bodhidharma was well versed in the martial arts of his homeland, and was a much respected member of a warrior caste. In his middle years

Bodhidharma for some reason renounced his birthright, took up the robes of priesthood and set off on a life in pursuit of truth and knowledge. History records that some years later Bodhidharma surfaced in Honan province, having crossed the seemingly impenetrable barrier of the Himalayas on foot. He came to a monastery named Shaolin where he found the monks in an emaciated state. According to legend, Bodhidharma introduced the monks to a series of exercises in an effort to get them fit and well. The 18 exercises he taught them were for conditioning the body and developing the mind. These therapeutic movements are popularly believed to be the forerunners of Shaolin temple boxing, known as the 18 Hands of Lo-Han.

Bodhidharma also brought Buddhist teachings and philosophies to these monks. It is believed that the Shaolin temple was the birthplace of the Ch'an philosophies, popularly known in the West as Zen.

The System Expanded

For 500 years or more, the Shaolin monks of Honan were feared as extraordinary fighters. They were men who, if they had to, could kill with their bare hands, although they upheld the Buddhist reverence for all forms of life. The only exception to this was in a life or death situation, when it was kill or be killed.

In 1589 a Chinese named Kwok Yuen entered the temple and expanded Bodhidharma's 18 exercises to 72. To increase the number of fighting systems Kwok Yuen disguised himself as an old man and wandered around the country in search of skilled teachers of kung fu. Upon his return to the temple with new instructors, the Shaolin boxing system was expanded even further, bringing the number of movements up to 170. These were then classified into five distinct styles: tiger, crane, leopard, snake, and dragon. Later, these individual styles were improved into a more effective system known as the *Five Animals Fist*.

The Test of Courage

Whenever a young monk undergoing training at Shaolin was thought ready to leave, having mastered all the kung fu skills, he had to take a life-or-death test. According to legend there were only two doors to the temple: the side door, which gave exit from and entry to the grounds, and the main entrance, which was only used by masters upon leaving. The candidate, in order to prove that he was a master of kung fu, had to make his way to this exit via a specially designed labyrinth filled with all manner of traps and dangerous obstacles designed to test his skills to the utmost. If the candidate failed the test, he would die in the tunnels and never be heard of again. The successful candidate, having mastered all the perils of the labyrinth, would eventually emerge at the front gate only to find it blocked by a huge smoldering metal urn. He had to move his last obstacle before gaining his freedom.

Because of its weight, the monk would have to bare his forearms and grasp the urn in his arms to lift it out of the way. In doing so, the front gate would be triggered open. Each side of the urn had a dragon carved on it. As the monk lifted this obstacle, he would be branded by the red-hot metal with the mark of the dragons on his forearms. This signified to everyone that the man marked with the twin dragons was a fighting priest of Shaolin, and a master of kung fu.

Understanding the Principles of Kung Fu

To achieve the slightest understanding of kung fu, a person has to be familiar with the underlying principles and constant theme of the Chinese martial arts. Most methods of kung fu appear to encompass philosophies based on nature, religion, and cosmology. Fighting techniques have been adapted from mammals, birds, insects, and even the tidal flow. A symbol that is seen inside kung fu *kwoons* (schools) all over the world is the *Yin-Yang*. This famous symbol, surrounded by eight trigrams, figuratively expresses nature and its changes. It is also known as the double fish symbol, representing opposites residing together. In the heart of Yin, the negative force of cold, darkness, and emptiness, is a tiny part of Yang — which is warmth, light, and positive energy. And in the heart of Yang is a small part of Yin.

This indicates that within strength is found weakness; within hardness, softness; and activity within inactivity. These alternating forces are indestructible and inexhaustible. They contradict as well as complement each other. The Chinese believe that without understanding this eternal duality one can never comprehend the true essence of kung fu, or the power that regulates the very universe itself.

The Two Basic Schools of Kung Fu

Chinese martial arts are generally divided into two broad approaches: one is the internal or soft school, and the other is the external or hard school. The internal encompasses the martial arts of pa-kua, hsing-i, and tai chi chuan. These Chinese boxing arts stress the metaphysical and philosophical aspects. The external systems are associated with Shaolin *chuan-fa* (Shaolin Fist), Hung Gar, and Tong Long. These schools stress power strikes, hand and body conditioning, and utilize force in straight lines, with much more emphasis on kicking.

The internal schools are usually considered to be defensive and passive, whereas the external systems are often more aggressive and muscular in approach.

The recurring theme throughout the oriental martial arts is that of religion. Both Buddhism and Taoism believe in attaining salvation through the cultivation of harmony in mind and body.

Chinese boxing, or kung fu, evolved into five major styles named for their creators — Hung, Lau, Monk, Choy, and Li. The many changes that these styles have gone through over the ages have resulted in the kung fu schools that we know today.

The Family System

The study and practice of kung fu in China built strong schools that were bound together like a family structure. The *sifu* (teacher) resembled the father figure, and the *sihings* (advanced students) were looked upon as older brothers. The novices and beginners were classed as younger brothers. Everyone in the school worked under a system based on self-discipline and sacrifice to perfect his art to the best of his ability. It is through this dedication and training that the arts of kung fu have survived the turbulent history of ancient China, to become a significant and vital aspect of today's martial arts.

The External or Hard Schools of Kung Fu

From the legacy handed down by the Shaolin monastery, many styles of kung fu have developed. The original five animals have been expanded many times over.

At a conservative estimate, there are about 1500 distinct kung fu styles practiced today, although many are still guarded with secrecy on mainland China.

It is only during the past 10 years or so that Chinese teachers have come out into the open and taught Westerners their art. At one time only Chinese would be accepted into the student ranks. They were known as 'closed door students'. In the early 1960s, a Westerner had to be something very special to warrant instruction from a Chinese master.

All of the kung fu styles combined undoubtedly hold the key to every possible defensive and offensive movement within their systems. Because it takes many years to complete just one of those systems, nobody can know everything. As a result each practitioner of kung fu always believes his system to be the best, and that as such it can beat all others. This gave rise to much in-fighting between rival schools. And even today in Hong Kong there are at least two to three bouts of *kong sau* (secret fights) every week in an effort to gain supremacy over a rival school of kung fu.

All the kung fu systems have their special merits, but there is no one system that is superior to all the rest. Many masters have come up with special movements based on all manner of fauna, but they still contain potential flaws or restrictions.

Hung Gar Chuan

Of the external styles, one of the most popular is hung gar chuan. *Hung* is the name of the originator, *gar* means 'family', and *chuan* means 'fist'. This is a southern Chinese style and was adapted from the Shaolin Tiger system. It incorporates the White Crane style and emphasizes very low, strong horse stances. Novices are supposed to stand in the horse stance practicing punching for three hours every day for three years before they are allowed to continue with further techniques. The system is said to possess a thrust punch that always results in a knockout.

Left *The horse stance of Hung Gar — the rigid and strong posture required by all practitioners of this art.*

Right *A master of wing chun kung fu adopting a typical kicking stance. In the practice of this art no kick is ever delivered above the belt.*

Praying Mantis or Tong Long

Legend has it that a kung fu master named Wang Lang went to the Shaolin temple to challenge the monks to a fight because he had heard that these monks were undefeatable. After receiving persistent challenges, the abbot sent out a novice monk to fight him. Within seconds, the novitiate monk had thrown Wang Lang to the ground and decisively defeated him. Building himself up with superior techniques, Wang Lang twice more went back to Shaolin to fight the monks, only to return each time bitterly defeated. Wang Lang retired in seclusion to the mountains and one day while sitting under a tree, he watched a fight between a grasshopper and a praying mantis. Although the grasshopper was bigger and stronger, it could not overcome the smaller and weaker mantis. Eventually the grasshopper was beaten and devoured by the praying mantis. Highly impressed by what he had seen, Wang Lang teased the mantis with a piece of long grass and memorised every defense and attack movement the mantis made. Wang Lang proceeded to devise a fighting system based on the movements of that little praying mantis. Returning to Shaolin, he issued the same challenge yet again, and this time Wang Lang defeated all comers.

The most distinctive movement in the mantis or tong long system is that of the mantis hand, which when attacking is shaped like a hook and looks like the insect's doubled-up forelegs. The fast footwork is based on the hops executed by the long-legged mantis.

Choy Lee Fut

In 1836 Chan Heung founded the system of kung fu called choy-lee-fut. The style was named after his two teachers Lee Yau-Shan and Choi Fok. *Fut* means 'Buddha' in Chinese. In his early years Chan fought against the British in the opium wars. He taught his kung fu to local villagers, in the hopes of forming a militia but, beaten by the British after one of the many uprisings, he fled to Nanking. There he set up one of the many tong and triad societies that flourished at that time. In his later years he went to America, settling in San Francisco, where he opened a kung fu kwoon.

Choy-lee-fut is one of the most popular kung fu styles in the United States. It is an all-purpose fighting art that uses grabbing and seizing methods. Punching is distinctive because of its long circular strikes, the blows being released only a foot away from the target. A student of this style attacks by running straight into an opponent and unleashing a whirlwind of overpowering hooks and uppercuts.

Wing Chun

Thanks to the late Bruce Lee, wing chun is probably the best known of all kung fu styles, because Lee looked to wing chun to form the nucleus of his own style of jeet kune-do. Wing chun originated in central China some 400 years ago. It was founded by a nun named Yim Wing Chun, who thought that the style she was learning at the time from her

Left *The practice of wing chun involves many very close-quarter strikes and blocks. Seen here the opponent has struck but the blow has been blocked and his own energy used to pull him forward onto an elbow strike to the face.*

Right *Action from the Bruce Lee movie 'Enter The Dragon'. This was the first film made by Bruce Lee for the US market and soon led to worldwide popularity.*

Above and right *A kung fu master employing the first principle of wing chun, which is economy of motion. This involves using the opponent's energy to redirect an attack, and turn it against him.*

Far right *The mook joong, better known as the wooden man of kung fu, is used to practice wrist hooks and hand blocking techniques. The wooden leg projecting from the bottom is used for perfecting kicks.*

teacher Ng Mui, was far too complex, and placed too much reliance on power techniques. As a result, she founded her own system. *Wing chun* means 'beautiful springtime'. It is a brutally effective combat system, based on economy of movement.

An adept of wing chun concentrates on defending his center line. This is an imaginary line running through the center of his body, where all the vital organs lie. The overall simplicity of wing chun is evident by the number of workable techniques involved in learning the system. There are only three forms to learn in order to gain mastery. Even the weapons system is limited to just two implements — the butterfly knives, and the six-and-a-half-point pole.

Wooden Dummy

In modern times the pioneer of wing chun was undoubtedly the grand master Yip Man. To enable students to fight with control, a unique training device in the shape of a wooden human being was constructed. Although the wooden dummy techniques are designed for advanced students, regular practice by intermediate students results in increased power. These 108 hand and kicking techniques are the hallmarks of the wing chun system.

Other Styles

Within the range of Chinese fighting systems come all manner of weird and wonderful titles — drunken man boxing, the white eyebrow, *fu jow pai* (tiger claw), monkey boxing, hop gar — the list is endless. Even mythical animals such as the dragon and the unicorn have given their names to fighting styles. Today in Hong Kong there are certain kung fu systems that up to the present time have never been taught to anyone who is not of pure Chinese blood.

The Boxer Uprising

The rebellion that took place in China in 1900 was known as the Boxer Rebellion. It was an uprising against the spread of Western influence, and was led by Ts'ao fu-T'ien. The term 'boxer' was applied by the British because of the many kung fu fighters who participated in the revolt. Many of the fighters belonged to a number of secret societies, the most famous of which was the I-Ho-Chuan, or the Society of Righteous and Harmonious Fists. These Chinese boxers achieved a reputation for almost supernatural strength and endurance. Many Chinese believed that their powers of kung fu would be far superior to the modern weapons of the Westerners.

The Death Touch

It is widely believed among many practitioners of kung fu that if the body is struck at a certain time of day, in some vital area in a certain manner, a chain reaction would start within the body, delaying the effect of the blow for anything up to a few months. After that the victim would die. This is known as *dim mak*, or 'the death touch'. It is a very controversial subject even among kung fu masters. The principle is supposed to work on the same lines as acupuncture. The assassin strikes, the victim feels no immediate effects, and thinks he is unharmed. But in a few days' or weeks' time he dies or becomes seriously ill. The majority of the tien hsueh arts (dim mak) are almost extinct. Only a handful of masters still possess the complete methods, and none of them is willing to part with the knowledge.

The Lion Dance

In the Chinese calendar, the New Year falls anytime between the end of January and mid-February. It is celebrated with much dancing and festivity. On these occasions a ritualistic dance, called the lion dance, is performed. This dance has been in existence for more than 1,000 years, and has very strict rules governing it. Traditionally the only people allowed to perform the dance were students of kung fu.

The Chinese regard the lion as an omen of good luck and prosperity, as distinct from other animals of the cat family. The lion is always classed as a peaceful friendly creature, and that is probably why no kung fu system has ever included the lion. Because of the lion's attributes, statues to it can be found all over China in front of stately palaces and shrines. Two guardian lions stood either side of the famed Shaolin temple, at the gateway. Whenever there is a festive day or a ceremonial event, the Chinese celebrate with the lion dance.

The head of the model lion can weigh in excess of 90 pounds so great stamina is needed to wield the head during the dance. That is why only advanced kung fu students are allowed to perform the dance. Accompanying the lion is its guide, known as dai tao fat. He wears a big mask, and holds a huge fan, and acts like a clown.

The Internal or Soft Schools of Kung Fu

In the 13th century in China, there lived a taoist monk named Chang San Feng. Growing a little disinterested in the martial arts of the day, he retired to the mountains to seek wisdom and knowledge. One night Cheng dreamt that God himself had taught him how to fight. The dream bothered the old monk and he spent many days pondering the meaning of it. Realization came as he watched a crane and a snake battling for supremacy. Neither could gain the advantage. Fascinated by the scene, the monk went on to study the techniques of these animals. When the crane attacked, the snake would outmaneuver the bird by twisting and turning. Likewise, when the snake attacked, the crane would lift its feet, flap its wings, and go perch on the limb of a tree.

Below: *Chinese lions from Kiang Chow province on mainland China. Traditionally, the lion dance is performed by practitioners of kung fu.*

Right: *Because wing chun is involved with close-in fighting, a strong defense is needed to protect the vulnerable centerline, where it is said all the vital points of the body exist.*

Chang saw that, unlike external systems where an attack was met by equal force, this fighting concept of the strong becoming yielding and the yielding becoming the strong, was completely new. He came to understand that counting on superior power to defeat an opponent was not enough in itself, and was perhaps even contrary to the laws of nature.

Continued studies showed Chang that force begets force, and often the best way to overcome force was not to fight it at all. The premise behind his new 'soft style' was simply to maximize internal energy through tranquility and thus minimize wasted external energy.

Tai-Chi Chuan

Translated as the 'grand or great ultimate fist' tai-chi chuan is one of the three major styles of kung fu in the internal school. Although tai-chi, as it is commonly called, is a form of Chinese boxing, with all its movements based on self-defense, it is because of its health aspect that practitioners are adopting this style of kung fu. The quite phenomenal boom across the United States of open-air tai-chi classes can only be compared with the similar popularity of Jane Fonda's aerobics some years ago.

Tai-chi is sometimes called moving meditation. It is steeped in philosophy and based on the principles of the Chinese classic, the *I-Ching* by Lao Tzu. The movements are continuous; there is no break from one to another and the practitioner is continually striving to push forward. The therapeutic benefits of the tai-chi form affect young and old alike. So startling have been the health improvements after six months of training in tai-chi that the authorities are now carrying out extensive research to discover why this ancient Chinese combat form is benefiting millions of

people in America in the 1980s. In the past few years research has shown that daily practice of the tai-chi form combats stress and anxiety at every level. Some big companies have even gone so far as to send its executives to classes to help them minimize mental fatigue and stress. The benefits of tai-chi are spread right across the board. Old people in Los Angeles and San Francisco have been given a new lease on life since taking up tai-chi. It has even been reported by one tai-chi group that a number of senior citizens enrolled in a class, the majority of whom were in wheelchairs. Within four months of learning the form, they had left their wheelchairs at home and were standing on their own without support, doing tai-chi.

The dreamlike dance movements of the tai-chi form are almost hypnotic. The exercise is performed quite literally in slow motion. It stresses tranquility in the midst of movement. The idea is to become like water and flow, envelop. The object of tai-chi is to unite mind and body in a state of complete harmony.

Tai-Chi in Combat

Tai-chi makes use of stillness in movement to contain movement. In its combat form, you wait for the other person to move and then you harness their force. When you do tai-chi you should be relaxed but not limp. This is softness on the outside but energy or hardness within, like an iron bar wrapped in cotton. The concept of defense in tai-chi is really quite simple. The attacker attacks, and without moving, the defender absorbs his direct energy and then repulses it. This direct force hitting the assailant head-on sends him sailing backwards through the air for as far as perhaps 20 feet.

Previous pages, left *Tai-Chi Chuan practitioners training in a Shanghai park . Millions of Chinese train in this martial art everyday.*

Previous pages, right *The stillness within movement of the tai-chi form, which promotes health and longevity. The movements in this sequence come from the Chen style of tai chi.*

Above *This pak mei instructor commands a veritable presence just by his physique alone. Some pak mei stances can be converted from open hands to fist forms instantly. The open hand can block then convert into a fist strike.*

Left *The claw-like hand formation is distinctive of pak mei kung fu.*

Using an X block this pak mei instructor effectively blocks a front kick to the groin. The X block can then be pushed upwards to take the attacker completely off his feet.

Pa-Kua

Pa-kua is the second of the internal forms of kung fu. The word means 'eight trigrams', and like tai-chi it is also based on the *I-Ching*. The style is based on the premise that if you can defend yourself at the eight compass points covered by the trigrams you will be fully protected from attack. Pa-Kua has many open-palm techniques for striking, and the footwork is based on the circle. When an attack is made, the aggressor is likely to find that his victim has avoided his blow and has got around behind him in order to retaliate.

Hsing-I

Hsing-I is the least common of the internal arts. it was created by a Chinese warrior named Yueh Fei in the 12th century. The art stresses the complementary principle of yin-yang, of both hard and soft, although the movements are very graceful. The *I* in Hsing-I means 'mind' or 'will'. So when you strike, you strike with your mind, although it is the forceful vertical attacks that do the damage. The five basic movements are based on the Chinese five elements of metal, water, wood, fire, and earth.

Legends of the Masters

In folklore the world over fanciful stories have emerged about heroes whose deeds defy the imagination. The annals of kung fu are rife with such tales. There was for example, the old monk named Hung Yun who lived in China during the Ming dynasty. In an effort to gain entrance to a certain monastery, he humbled himself by waiting outside the gates all day and all night in a raging blizzard. When he was brought in unconcious the next morning, drops of his blood fell on the earth outside. As the sun rose, the blood formed a red mist and floated across the sky. When his helpers saw this, they named him *Hung Yun*, which means 'Red Cloud'. Hung later went on to found the tien shan pai system of kung fu, and his followers helped to stiffen Chinese resistance to the Manchurians and their Ching dynasty.

Then there is the story of the Tibetan lama who was disturbed while meditating by a lake. Turning around he saw a white crane and a huge ape locked in combat. It seemed almost certain that the crane would die as the ape gripped the bird with its massive paws, but the crane maneuvered its body away from the ape's grip, and instead of fleeing, fought back with equal ferocity. Using its powerful wings for balance, it made repeated charges at the ape with its rapierlike beak poking at the vulnerable spots on the ape's body. Eventually the ape, after losing an eye fled to the shelter of the forest. The lama was so fascinated by what he had just witnessed that he went on to study the movements of the crane, and founded a kung fu system around it, naming the system for the crane.

Monks and holy men in kung fu folklore are always the central characters of the stories. This is because it was only those seekers of knowledge who had the time to formulate ideas. One old monk, who invented a very famous style of kung fu, was actually thrown out of the Shaolin temple. Bok Mei, as he was called, had a long white beard, long white hair, and huge eyebrows. While learning the skills of kung fu at Shaolin, he killed a fellow disciple. Because of this, even though it was an accident, he was expelled from the monastery with orders never to return. Bok Mei left and sought refuge in the mountains. As a result of his observations of nature, he created a style designed mainly for speed. It later became known as 'the white eyebrow style' named for him. But Bok Mei's mistake was never forgotten at Shaolin and his style was banned by members of the Shaolin temple.

The Impact of Bruce Lee

Even to non-followers of the martial arts, the name of Bruce Lee is synonymous with spectacular fight scenes, amazing flying kicks, and the use of bare hands against all kinds of weapons and opponents. He was given the title 'The King Of Kung Fu', and there is no doubt that the emergence of Bruce Lee onto the martial arts movie scene created a box

The man who started it all, the late great Bruce Lee. This and following page, left A scene from 'Enter The Dragon'. Right Bruce Lee in a typical pose with the Chinese nunchaku under his armpit ready to strike. Kung fu movies led to the notoriety of the awesomely effective nunchaku.

Following page, right One of Bruce Lee fans' favorite poses — with his nunchakus held high.

office sensation that not only swept the country but the world. This, coupled with David Carradine and his hit 'kung fu' series, set the wheels in motion for the kung fu boom of the early 1970s.

Bruce Lee, the Man

Bruce Lee was the son of a touring Chinese opera star. He was born in San Francisco and raised in Hong Kong. When he was 18 he returned to the United States to further his education at the University of Washington. Already well versed in kung fu, which he had learned in his formative years in Hong Kong, he was accepted to play the role of Kato in television's *Green Hornet* series. Although the series did not prove to be a huge success in the US, the dubbed version, screened in Hong Kong, set Lee on the road to fame

and fortune. Chinese producer Raymond Chow offered him a part in the movie *The Big Boss*. This was a hit, and Lee went on to make more kung fu films. Because Bruce Lee was a committed martial artist, he would not be led into silly fight scenes. Instead, he insisted on realism, and even choreographed many of the fight sequences himself.

But it was in the movie *Enter the Dragon* that Bruce Lee really made his name. It put him in the million-dollar bracket and the box office records list.

Jeet Kune-Do

Having learned wing chun kung fu in his youth, Bruce Lee went on to formulate his own system, which he called *jeet kune-do,* or 'way of the intercepting fist'. Hollywood stars flocked to him for private lessons. James Coburn, who was

already interested in karate, went over to learn Bruce Lee's system, as did the late Steve McQueen.

During this successful period, Lee was beginning to open up new horizons in his own expression of kung fu. He still felt limited within his martial arts and thought that if a fighting system was to be any good it shouldn't have any limits at all.

Bruce Lee drove himself beyond the limits of endurance to perfect and try out his jeet kune-do method of fighting. His punishing routine, plus the pressure of his movie obligations, drove Bruce Lee to the very brink, but still he worked on, even harder.

The Little Pill that Killed a Giant

At the very height of his film career and popularity, Bruce Lee died. Earlier in a strange prophecy, he had told his wife Linda that he didn't know how much longer he could keep it all up. The hectic pace was beginning to tell.

Bruce Lee's sudden death on 20th July 1973 shocked the world. The Chinese press went to town with innuendo and rumor of how the king of kung fu had died. Every theory in the book was put forward, from assassination to his having fallen foul of a triad society. As a result, he had suffered the fabled delayed 'death touch'.

The inquest disclosed that Bruce Lee had died from an edema of the brain, caused by a painkilling drug known as equagesic, to which he was allergic. The little dragon as Lee was known to the Chinese, had been downed by a tiny pill.

Although Bruce Lee's untimely death was felt the world over, the legacy he left inspired martial artists everywhere.

The Breaking Energy of Kung Fu

Just as the karate adept has the capability of breaking objects, so too has kung fu. To break any object with force requires a great deal of strength. When a kung fu practitioner is faced with something to be broken, he summons up a powerful unseen force that lies within him. This intrinsic energy, or vital air, is called *Chi*. Chi energy is developed in virtually every kung fu style practiced today. Some adepts even make a lifelong pursuit of cultivating this force within the body.

The study of this art is known as chi-gung. Apart from giving its user phenomenal strength, it bequeathes to its practitioners good health, sound blood circulation, and a youthful appearance. It is basically a special breathing exercise, but has many complex mental aspects. A master of chi-gung can, at any given moment, direct this invisible energy to any part of his body. In demonstrations, a master has held his hands palms uppermost, and within minutes his hands have began to radiate heat — not just warmth but real heat.

In order to develop this chi energy, great concentration is required. It has been said that masters in ancient China could summon their chi so quickly and direct it to any part of the body, that if they were attacked with a bladed weapon, the blade would not be able to penetrate the skin. Even in modern times demonstrations using sharpened meat cleavers have been seen. A member of the audience has attempted to cut through a chi-gung master's skin with a cleaver, but after five minutes or so, after making no impression, has given up.

Amazing Techniques of Chi-Gung

One of the hardest materials to break is stone. Manufactured sidewalk pavings and house bricks can all be broken with a fair amount of pressure and know-how. But a rounded stone formed in the earth is another ball game altogether. At a recent kung fu demonstration, a master not only broke a stone using the side of his hand, but he also sliced the stone into three pieces, much to the amazement of his audience.

Other astounding feats abound in the martial arts world. There was the case of the slim young lady lying on her back and allowing a 200-pound man to jump off a table and land with both feet squarely on her tummy. By directing her chi to that area, she resisted the impact without harm. In another demonstration, a small bed of nails was placed sharp end down on a practitioner's stomach, while he lay prone. Then seven house bricks were stacked on top of the bed of nails. One of the master's students took a huge hammer and began to pound at the bricks, until everyone of them was broken. Clearing away the debris, the master calmly rose to his feet, moved the bed of nails away from his stomach, and showed that there was not a mark on him — not even the slightest indentation.

Left *Using chi gung energy a kung fu master has two roofing tiles smashed against his ribs.* Middle *Using their inherent internal energy two chi gung adepts bend a thick iron wire against their throats.* Below *With a head strike a kung fu master smashes his way through four two-inch-thick concrete slabs. All these highly dangerous techniques should never be attempted by an unqualified person.*

Left *Mike Dayton has honed his chi gung powers to extraordinary levels. Here he successfully breaks out of a pair of steel handcuffs.*

In a chi-gung mind control exercise, another master stacked up five bricks, and announced that he would break all of them except the middle one. Sure enough, when the break was done, all the bricks crumbled into dust — all that is, except the specified middle one. Feats such as these have to be witnessed to be fully appreciated.

In Manchester, England, a Thai boxing master walked onto the demonstration floor at a national tournament. He placed a large wooden board on the floor, opened a bag containing about half-a-dozen Coca Cola bottles, and began to break them with a hammer. The broken glass spread all over the board, the sharp jagged ends sticking up into the air. Standing up, the master then poured gasoline over the broken bottles and set the whole lot alight. Calmly he walked into this inferno of glass and flames and began to perform techniques. In one such movement he raised his leg into the air way above his head. The supporting leg scrunched sickeningly into the jagged glass, with flames leaping and dancing over the flesh. After about two minutes he stepped off the burning glass with not a mark, cut, or burn on his person. How can it be explained? Some people describe such demonstrations as sensational tricks. But if they defy the laws of science, can they be called tricks?

The Wu Shu of Mainland China

One form of kung fu that is daily practiced by more than a hundred million people, is wu shu, or martial art of China, as it is more correctly termed.

Since the communist revolution in mainland China, the practice of kung fu has become part of the everyday school curriculum on mainland China, although strictly speaking, the martial arts as we know them bear little resemblance to the gymnastics as practiced in Peking. Wu shu is regarded as a traditional sport form and physical culture, and as such falls into two basic categories. Boxing and grappling form one, and the play of weapons makes up the other. The splendid colorful uniforms and gymnastic routines do not make up for the sad fact that this is what the Chinese mainland feels kung fu is all about.

Traditional weaponry and its usage play a very big part in wu shu. Items such as the three-section staff, the double hooks, the nine-section whip, the iron fan, and the long tasselled sword are just a few of the weapons used. Wu shu has been described as a showbiz sport, where no one gets hurt but which leaves the audience spellbound. In 1974 a touring world wu shu team visited the United States in a cultural exchange program. It gave performances in San Francisco, Washington DC and New York.

A classic pose of wu shu swordplay using the wu shu jien or sword. It is a fine example of a martial art taken to its purest form.

On mainland China, children begin to practice wu shu from an early age. In the grounds of the Shanghai Palace, children perform sword and spear movements.

Left *Students from a wu shu school in Tientsin province on mainland China show their skill and artistry fighting with spear and broadsword.*

53

The super power of chi gung seems to know no boundaries. Even wu shu has its own exponents of this amazing inner strength. Left: A master smashes a razor-sharp broadsword against his bare skin without even a cut. Below: A fine-point spear is pushed against the throat of a chi gung practitioner without any apparent harm.

Right Age is no barrier when it comes to learning kung fu. And any weapon can be adapted to beat off an attacker.

Kung Fu Facts and Fancy

Fallacies about kung fu, when related by the ill-informed, are often taken as gospel. So it is time that some of these myths were dispelled.

It has been said that world heavyweight boxing champion Muhammad Ali was never beaten outside the ring by a kung fu man. What actually happened was that while Muhammad Ali was visiting Singapore, at the height of his fame, he was asked to punch a kung fu practitioner named Wong Yue Chee in the throat, as part of a demonstration of chi-gung. Ali complied and was amazed to see that the blow had no effect on Wong Yue Chee.

There was a rumor that Adolf Hitler knew about and perhaps studied kung fu. The facts are that in 1936 at the Olympic Games in Berlin he had the opportunity to watch some of China's top kung fu players perform. They came from the Nanking Central Kung Fu Academy. Hitler was quoted as saying that he was very impressed with Chinese kung fu.

Gung fu is not another martial art but is merely the Cantonese pronunciation of kung fu.

The Shaolin temple in Honan was not the only temple where kung fu was practiced. In fact, there were numerous temples in and around China named Shaolin, and most of them had thriving kung fu classes.

Though the two religions of Taoism and Buddhism were equally popular, Shaolin was strictly Buddhist. The Taoist temple was named Wa Lum, and was located in Shantung. The name Sil Lum is Cantonese for Shaolin, and not another monastery, as some people believe.

The five ancestors generally regarded as the founders of the present-day Triad societies were survivors of the Shaolin temple after it had been burnt and sacked by the Ching emperor's army. Out of the 128 resident monks, 110 perished in the flames. The 18 survivors fled, but 13 of them were caught and killed. The remaining five managed to cross the Yellow River and escape.

Hollywood Catches the Kung Fu Bug

With the death of Bruce Lee, and the television *Kung Fu* series breaking all records in the ratings, the Hollywood movie machine slipped into top gear. A proliferation of movies, all concerned in some way with martial arts, filled the screens across the country. Top kung fu and karate instructors were being screen-tested to see if they could fill the slot made vacant by Bruce Lee's untimely death. David Carradine, already assured of fame from his hit series, went on to make a martial arts movie that had been scripted by Bruce Lee himself, called *The Silent Flute*. Nick Hammond, alias Spiderman, brought martial arts to the kids, via the cartoon hero. Ron Ely did all his own martial arts work in the Tarzan TV series. In 1980 a young Chinese star arrived in the United States to make a film called *The Big Brawl*. His name was Jackie Chan. He brought humor and comedy into kung fu movies, and was even dubbed the new Bruce Lee.

Eventually, as all fads do, these faded away. But thanks to the initial kung fu boom of the 1970s, movie producers and directors had been educated to appreciate what real fight scenes were all about. Today's film industry and television, both use accredited martial arts choreographers for their fight scenes. After all, that's what the public wants to see.

Iron Palm

A lethal practice in kung fu is a specialized technique known as iron palm. Its practitioner can kill with a single blow. The entire forearm must be conditioned gradually over a period of several years. Training for this technique involves punching bags filled with sand, then later with pebbles and finally with iron filings or metal shot. To aid a student of iron palm in his build-up of hand conditioning, a special ointment is used called dit da jow, made from an ancient recipe. Handed down in Chinese families from generation to generation, it is applied externally, after first being heated. It is said to help prevent bruising and internal injuries, while at the same time strengthening the skin, muscles, and bone. No iron palm practitioner would attempt to train without first using this ointment.

Chinese Medicine

It is not uncommon to find that most masters of kung fu are also accomplished doctors of traditional Chinese herbal medicine. Medication, bone-setting, and massage all go hand-in-hand with kung fu. Many teachers have also studied acupuncture, and are well versed in the ailments of the human body.

Jiu Jitsu Judo Aikido

*Seek not to know the answers
but to understand the questions.*

Left *At a Japanese dojo, a young judoka
(student) receives his yellow belt from his
sensei (teacher). The scroll indicates that he
has passed a certain kyu (grade).*

Right *The attacker has taken his opponent's
legs away with a foot sweep, then turned him
to send him crashing to the floor.*

In the traditional martial arts systems, the warrior would only grapple if all else failed. The classical warrior fought in armor, so the empty hand skills looked a little robotic in their execution. When an unseated horseman was fighting without weapons, the warrior would unbalance his adversary and secure him with a lock or grip. This would give him enough time to pull out his short dagger, and thrust it through a chink in the armor to strike a vital point.

Jiu Jitsu

In Japan, between the 17th and 19th centuries, the Samurai began to fit into a more peaceful environment, devoid of the earlier bloody civil struggles. The Samurai often had trouble when attacked by bandits or lawless Samurai *(ronin)*. The need for empty hand techniques grew and, when the Samurai were forbidden to wear swords in 1876, it became imperative.

Jiu jitsu is an ancient Japanese martial art that includes both armed and unarmed techniques. It is regarded as the grandfather of aikido and judo. Jiu jitsu is first and foremost a method of combat, originally used by the Samurai. Within its system lies a variety of skills, from striking vital points and kicking, to strangling and joint locking techniques. It has been said that jiu jitsu was first practiced some 2000 years ago, and many believe it to be the father of all Japanese martial arts.

Modern Outlook

The emphasis in jiu jitsu today is on dislocation of a joint or limb by means of locks or leverage grips. In other words, exponents of the art don't go all the way. The locks are so complete in themselves that the mere threat of damage which their application implies, is sufficient to induce even the most hardened opponent to cry for mercy.

Jitsu means 'art' or 'skill' and *Jiu* means 'gentle' or 'soft'. Thus, freely translated, jiu jitsu is the gentle art, although

one would not think so to see skilled practitioners in Japan weighing a little more than 120 pounds throwing burly westerners about like rag dolls.

The Samurai

Jiu jitsu was as much a weapon of the Samurai as was the sword. They were trained in the techniques of arm locks and bone-breaking from a very early age. The fear of death had no place in the Samurai's heart, for he followed the code of *Bushido,* 'the Warrior Way'. Every Samurai was trained in the throws and grappling movements of jiu jitsu. The Samurai had special charts drawn up showing the vital areas of the human body, with the special one-punch killer blows marked out. These charts had been compiled over a period of time, and tested on condemned prisoners.

The Code of Bushido

All Samurai followed a strict code of discipline called *Bushido.* This was a moral code of loyalty, duty, and obedience, which had been developed to set a high standard in the training of warriors in the martial arts. It could be likened to the chivalrous code of the knights in feudal Europe. But in effect it was much more than this. The code was a guideline for the Samurais' daily behavior. Should a warrior step outside these rules, he would be expected to discipline himself accordingly, even to the supreme and ultimate act of committing *seppuku* (the formal name for *hari-kiri* or belly-cutting). To a Samurai, fighting was his only vocation, and in some cases it could even be described as an obsession.

Time Out from Fighting

When the warriors of feudal Japan weren't involved in one of the many wars of that period, they spent their leisure time immersed in martial activities, but for sporting purposes. But even then, the strict code still applied. They placed great emphasis on victory in combat, whether for real or not. It was not unusual for exponents to go to a sporting session and never return. Many deaths resulted from dangerous techniques used in these so-called leisure sports of the period.

Zen in the Martial Arts of Japan

The Zen Buddhist sect appealed most directly to the Samurai because it was a faith which taught that salvation came not from some faraway god but from within the individual himself. The idea that a man could influence his own destiny appealed to men who lived with warfare and death on a daily basis. The official religion at that time in Japan was Shinto, and the two religions coexisted with few

problems. But the influence of Zen Buddhism on Japanese martial ways in general was far-reaching.

Jiu Jitsu as a Sport

The classical Japanese martial arts are not sports. Although jiu jitsu is strictly a martial art, it has, over the last 10 years or so, been developed as a sporting and competitive activity. At world class level, because of its competitive aspects jiu jitsu has had to have many of its lethal techniques deleted because otherwise the worlds arenas would be littered with dead bodies.

Many staunch traditionalists refuse to take part in active competition because they feel that this modern concept is diluting the classical martial way of jiu jitsu.

Jiu Jitsu Styles

Scholars trace the development of jiu jitsu back to the old Japanese art of *sumo* in 23 BC. Ancient records document the existence of more than 700 distinct schools of jiu jitsu in feudal Japan. These ancient documents credit Takenuchi Hisamori with having first systemized jiu jitsu in 1532, when he founded Takenuchi-Ryu.

As with all martial arts the world over, offshoots from the original systems spring up. A popular style in the United States, called 'small circle jiu jitsu', was developed by Professor Wally Jay of Almeda, California.

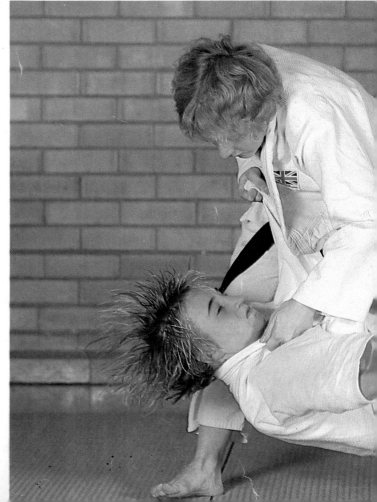

The popularity of judo amongst women has grown enormously since World War II. And now the women are as keen as the men in competition.

p61
Following pages, left *Neil Adams of the UK grips Kase of Japan in an armlock on the ground to take a gold medal in the World Judo Championships.* Following pages, right *More action from the competition arena. Judo enthusiasts are encouraged to take part in tournament competition from early stages in their training.*

Armed Forces Training

The art of jiu jitsu has been known to the Western world since the turn of the century. Government departments of law enforcement were quick to recognize the efficiency of an unarmed fighting style that was relatively easy and quick to learn. So gradually, the various agencies began to receive expert tuition in jiu jitsu. They formulated a training curriculum and taught their personnel the basic principles of jiu jitsu. At first, the army taught their recruits fundamental throws and locks, but with special services groups, techniques were gone into in greater depth.

World War Two

With the attack on Pearl Harbor, the United States was thrown headlong into the great conflict. The need for highly skilled operatives to carry out secret work behind enemy lines led the Pentagon to recruit second-generation Japanese Americans whose knowledge and skill in the darker side of the martial arts of Japan was unsurpassed.

Very soon these special service personnel were being instructed in the quick decisive strangulation techniques, used for killing sentries. The nerve point skills of *atemi-waza* for silent killing were also learnt. Within a few weeks American special agents from the OSS went out into the field, armed with a whole arsenal of deadly unarmed combat skills to aid them in their special work.

61

Resuscitation Skills

Strangely enough, when learning the classical art of jiu jitsu, an exponent has to go through the full range of movements and techniques. He has to learn how to strangle and dislocate, how to break limbs and throw adversaries three times his own weight before he is taught the secret art, which is the skill of resuscitating an opponent. This special skill is known as *kuatsu*. The reasoning behind leaving resuscitation skills until the end is that jiu jitsu was formulated as a battlefield killing art, and as such, the priority is to kill. If an opponent were to half kill his adversary, then change his mind because he might have wanted to question him first, he could resuscitate him, using one of the many methods he had been taught. Even today, this special training is still reserved for only the most senior of jiu jitsu practitioners.

Judo

Judo is the modern sports form of jiu jitsu. It was developed by Professor Jigoro Kano in 1882 in Suidobashi, Tokyo. It is a well organized system of unarmed techniques, primarily based on leverage throws and holds. Judo is not a jitsu art, the word *judo* meaning 'gentle way'. It is a form of sport rather than any kind of martial art involving death or serious injury.

Fundamentals of the Sport

A person trained in judo has the skill and ability to beat another equally or more highly skilled player in competition. One who practices the skill of judo, is called a *Judoka*. The method of winning in competition is defined in a mutually accepted system of rules laid down by the organizing body. Judo has the distinction of being the only oriental martial art to be accepted by the Olympic Games, although in the 1988 games to be held at Seoul in South Korea it is assumed that Korea's own national sport of *taekwon-do* will be admitted to the lists.

Judo Established in America

Judo's beginnings in the United States resulted from the influx of Japanese immigrants into the country. It was in the Japanese communities on the west coast, notably in Los Angeles and San Francisco, that judo first got started. Just off downtown Los Angeles near to City Hall, lies an area known as Little Tokyo. It was there that a Japanese judo First Dan named Nina founded the first dojo. Today that same block is occupied by the headquarters of the Los Angeles Police Department. Nina's club opened in 1909 with about seven practicing students.

By 1920 the first judo tournaments were being staged. It was during this period that most of the men who were later to become the really big names in American judo began to show up. There was Toshitaku Yamauchi, who went on to become an Eighth Dan, and founded judo in New York. Also on the scene at that time was Kiro Nagano, now also an Eighth Dan.

Judo at the White House

America's first real experience of judo came in 1902 when President Theodore Roosevelt took judo lessons in the White House from a Japanese Tenth Dan named Yamashita, who had arrived in the United States with a special Japanese delegation. Theodore Roosevelt, known for his 'try-anything' attitude was so impressed with this 'gentle art' that could enable a smaller man to hurl a six-foot 200-pound army sergeant clear across a room that he undertook to learn it. His daughter, who had also witnessed the prowess of this little Japanese during the impromptu demonstration, joined him. Through hard work, both Roosevelt and his daughter went on to become black belts.

Jiu Jitsu, Judo, Aikido

Judo Basics

Generally speaking, the first techniques taught in judo are the ones for falling without injuring oneself. These are called *ukemi waza* or breakfalls. A human being when falling down has a tendency to put out a hand to break the fall. In doing so, he stands a chance of fracturing or breaking his wrist. The two important things to remember are not to let the head hit the ground first and not to let the hands fly wildly in the air. Before any prospective judoka is allowed to learn anything about throwing he has to know how to breakfall correctly.

In a matted dojo in Japan young children watch with interest at the movements of their sensei as he puts a young judoka through his paces.

In competition, ladies' judo takes on a slightly different form from that of the men's section. But the competition is just as fierce.

65

Below *Great Britain's Neil Adams takes Lehman to the ground at the 1980 Moscow Olympics.*

Below *Denmark and Argentina meet on the competition floor.*

Below *Ground play in judo is as important as actually getting your man down there in the first place. In this tournament the judoka is going for what is known as an upper body pin. To facilitate this move the hands must be tight and strong but the body loose. So the protagonist can follow his opponent around easily and quickly, should he try to escape from the hold, the attacker's weight must be kept low so as to hinder his opponent in shifting ground.*

Left *A judoka in competition uses a lifting throw to turn his man and take him down. In tournaments, despite which grade or colour belt the man has achieved, in order to identify each fighter one man wears a white belt and the other a red belt.*

Below *Because competition judo is a little restrictive, many judo players prefer to keep safe and play tried and tested techniques.*

Most Titles in Judo

Since the first world judo championships were inaugurated in Tokyo on 5th May 1956, only two men have won most titles. Interestingly enough, one was an Oriental and the other a Westerner. Wilhelm Ruska of Holland took the 1967 and 1971 heavyweight titles, and also the 1972 Olympic heavyweight and open titles in Munich, West Germany. The Japanese with four titles was Shozo Fujii, who took the world championship middleweight division in 1971, 1973, 1975 and 1979.

When judo was first introduced into the Olympics in 1964 in Tokyo, the Japanese people were shocked when Dutchman Anton Geesink won the open title. When the women's championships were instituted in 1971, Christine Childs, a Fifth Dan from Great Britain, took the heavyweight title on six occasions.

Judo Facts

The belt colors used in judo, in order of increasing rank are red for absolute beginner, then white, yellow, orange, green, blue, brown, and black. Jigoro Kano, the founder of judo was a Twelfth Dan.

The suit a judoka wears is called a *Judogi*, and is made of heavy cotton so that it will not tear easily when pulled or grabbed. The belt is about nine feet long and is tied around the waist twice.

The world headquarters for judo and the acknowledged mecca is the Kodokan in Japan.

Aikido

Both judo and aikido have their origins in jiu jitsu. The founder of aikido, Morihei Ueshiba, was himself a high ranking jiu jitsu instructor. He took up jiu jitsu because in his teens he had been severely weakened as a result of scarlet fever. He had looked around for a martial art that would help to build him up again, and jiu jitsu, with its strong physical techniques, seemed ideal. But later on in life, it was these very same physical tendencies that Ueshiba became dissatisfied with. So he went on to found the discipline of aikido or 'The Way of all Harmony'.

The Aims of Aikido

Training in aikido differs from training in other Japanese martial arts. It is necessary to understand not only the unique movements and techniques of the art, but also the deep underlying philosophy that teaches adepts to master the mind, develop the character, and cultivate to a high degree the art of living in harmony with everyday circumstances. Aikido's primary objective is to unify mind,

During an aikido contest an opponent is thrown whilst the wrist remains trapped in order to further counter-attack if the man does not submit.

body, and the mysterious force known as *ki*. The ki is the very soul of aikido, and it can be loosely described as a super force or power that is inherent in every human being — a souped-up source of pure energy, waiting to be developed and then tapped.

Aikido in Action

Aikido techniques use an element of compliance such as is found in jiu jitsu. The attacker lunges forwards, so the defender, using his aikido skills, will harmonize with the movement and seek to redirect it. For instance, if someone were to pull at you, you can either resist, in which case the stronger of the two will prevail, or you can suddenly go in the direction you are being pulled. The effect of this is to unbalance the attacker, making him open to your next planned response.

The *aikidoka* (one skilled in aikido) performs his movements with a very fluid motion. To compete or fight in aikido takes much more skill than is found in any of the other striking martial arts.

Unlike judo and jiu jitsu, an aikido practitioner does not wear the traditional suit as seen in the other two arts. Instead, he wears a garb known as *hakama*, which is a long split skirt covering the legs down to the feet. One of the reasons for wearing the hakama is so that no one will be able to observe the foot movements.

The Mystic and the Ki

When the founder of Aikido was about 85 years old, he began to get the reputation of being something of a mystic, because of the many unexplainable feats he performed to demonstrate the power of the ki force within him.

On one occasion Ueshiba, who stood only five feet tall and weighed a mere 120 pounds, gave a demonstration of his art. In front of two dozen or so newspapermen, he called for six volunteers to attack him. Six men of various sizes and weights stepped up to accept the challenge. The great teacher told all men to attack him simultaneously. When they did so, the old man, hardly moving, sent his would be assailants flying in all directions.

Before the demonstration, Ueshiba had drawn a small chalk circle around his feet to prove to the onlookers that little movement was required to effect the technique. As the six men got up from the ground everyone looked to Ueshiba, whose feet still remained firmly planted within that circle.

Aikido makes use of circular wrist movements. The woman by pushing forward, can take her attacker down to the ground and yet still retain the wrist lock.

Martial Arts of the Orient

Tremendous energy flows through the aikidoist whilst performing his art.

Walking the Teacups

At another time, Ueshiba wanted to demonstrate the positive attitude that the ki force creates. He told an audience that he could will himself to become two-thirds lighter than his own body weight. He next took 20 teacups, filled them with tea, and arranged them with their saucers in a circle. Stepping up onto the rim of the first tea cup, he commenced to walk round the complete circle of cups, on the rims. When he had finished, no tea had been spilled in the saucers, and none of the delicate china cups had been cracked or broken. This, he explained, was ki in action.

The Unmoveable Man

A very famous story relating to Ueshiba, describes how, when in front of television cameras, he invited four men to see if they could lift him from the ground. Bearing in mind that Ueshiba was in his eighties and weighed little more than 120 pounds, this would seem an easy task. The old man stood silently and concentrated his ki energy downwards towards the ground. The four men walked up, put their arms around his waist and lifted. Try as they would, they could not budge this frail old man from the spot. Eventually, the four men decided that two would grab his feet, and two would lift him from the waist in one co-ordinated movement. And still they failed, much to their amazement. The old man remained rooted to the spot.

The Major Schools of Aikido

Although Morihei Ueshiba was the founder of modern aikido, there are more than 30 distinct styles of the art. Most founders of the other systems were pupils of the great Ueshiba. Kenji Tomiki was the first of Ueshiba's students to be awarded his Eighth Dan black belt. Tomiki aikido, named for him, is a style that stresses competition. He believed, unlike Ueshiba, that his students would gain mental improvement if they engaged in techniques during active freestyle competition. Another style is yoshinkan aikido, devised by Gozo Shioda, another former pupil of Ueshiba.

Yoshinkan style was the form the Tokyo police adopted for the training of their officers. Today Shioda has more than 200 black belt instructors teaching city police forces throughout Japan.

Aikido Conclusion

Although, on the face of it, aikido is a splendid system for self-defense, it is its deep philosophy of life that sets it apart from the other Japanese martial arts. The central aim of aikido is self-realization through discipline. This discipline begins with the learning of the correct use of physical energy in the aikido movements. Harmony of body and mind gradually develops with practice, and as the desire for immediate results falls away, the process of realization begins. It was the founder himself who said 'Aikido has no end — there's just the beginning and further growth'.

Taekwon-do
the art of Korea

A steed is not praised for its might,
but for its thoroughbred quality.
Confucius

Left *The son of the present-day grandmaster of hwarang-do, Joo Bang Lee, strikes up a classical pose of this ancient Korean martial art.*

Right *In a taekwon-do competition, a reverse back roundhouse kick strikes the opponent, who quickly counters the attack with a rising knee block.*

Following pages *A practitioner of taekwon-do executing a fine example of a full flying front kick. This kick was originally used to unseat warriors from their horses.*

Taekwon-do is a martial art which was developed independently centuries ago in Korea, although in those days it was known as tae kyon.

Tae means 'to kick or smash with the feet', and *kwon* means 'to punch or destroy with the hand or fist'. *Do* means 'method'.

Beginnings

Taekwon-do is the technique of unarmed combat for self-defense. It has more than 1300 years of history and tradition behind it. A Buddhist monk named Won Kwang is said to have originated the five principles that today form the basis of taekwon-do. The art developed as a means of self-protection for the scattered tribal groups who were under constant threat from their warlike neighbors.

The Three Kingdoms

In those days the Korean peninsula consisted of three kingdoms. The smallest of these was the Silla Kingdom, which was always under attack from its two powerful enemies to the north and west. Because of its geographical location it was also threatened from Japan. The constant raids led the nobility to form an elite group or army of fighting men to protect them.

The Hwarang

This elite fighting corps was called the *hwarang-do* or 'Way of the Flowering Manhood'. All the men were young, strong, and fit, the cream of Silla manhood. Apart from the regular military training they received, the Hwarang learned the disciplines of mind and body from the Buddhist priests. They voluntarily exposed themselves to severe hardships in order to condition themselves so they would become like steel.

Fighting, marching, training, all were done at treble the accepted normal pace until eventually this Hwarang army became more than a match for any invader, no matter how outnumbered they were.

Living Legends

Before long the deeds of the Hwarang became legendary, not only on the battlefields, but for the way they conducted their lives. They have often been compared with the Samurai warriors of Japan. Gradually, after gaining victory after victory, the Korean peninsula became unified under the banner of the Silla Kingdom. The people, inspired by the feats of their elite fighting men, began to adopt the unarmed fighting principles of taekwon-do. So popular did this art become, that it was soon turned into a sport and was a regular feature at athletic competitions and festivals.

The Golden Age

Towards the end of the 10th century the Kingdom of Silla because of internal dissension, was overthrown, and the Kingdom of the Koryo dynasty was founded. The Western name Korea comes from *Koryo*. Because this kingdom's survival still rested on maintaining a strong army, tae kyon or taekwon-do was openly and actively encouraged by the government. It eventually became compulsory for all young men, from age six upwards, to practice the art. Just as children in America today play baseball, the children of Korea used to practice the foot-smashing techniques of taekwon-do.

Taekwon-do Dies

For 500 years compulsory training in taekwon-do remained on the statute books of the Koryo government. Then came an era of enlightenment, and anything related to military training was scorned. So the rot had set in for this ancient fighting art. Many of the trained Buddhist monks went up into the mountains to become recluses, but they kept the art alive. By the time of the Japanese occupation in 1909 the art had almost died out. The Japanese put the final nail in its coffin by forbidding the practice of any kind of martial discipline.

Taekwon-do Emigrates

The few remaining stalwarts who possessed the knowledge of taekwon-do emigrated to China and Japan, looking for work and to start new lives. No restrictions on unarmed martial arts training existed in those countries.

Because of this emigration, taekwon-do became influenced slightly by other forms of martial arts. When Korea was liberated in 1945 many Koreans returned to their homeland bringing with them the refined and improved taekwon-do.

Modern Taekwon-do Emerges

For five years after World War Two, taekwon-do existed in Korea under various forms and titles. The advent of the Korean War brought a man named Choi Hong Hi onto the scene. Choi, a professional soldier, taught the old tae kyon system to his men and was eventually promoted to general in the Korean army. Through his military liaison with

foreign units, Choi spread the knowledge of his system until it became international. In 1954 Choi became head of the board concerned with the development of a unified martial art. His suggestion of the name taekwon-do for the national art of Korea was enthusiastically received and adopted.

Martial Arts Politics

In 1966 the first taekwon-do federation was formed on an international scale. A few years later, because of political pressure, Choi left the country. The Korean government quickly set up a rival organization to the ITF and called it the World Taekwon-do Federation. Today both these groups exist in their own spheres, although it can be said that the WTF is by far the larger of the two. It is hoped that as Taekwon-do is the national art and sport of Korea, it will be included in the 1988 Olympic Games, to be held in Seoul.

The United States and Taekwon-do

The Korean War had a tremendous influence on American servicemen, martial arts wise. The many thousands of soldiers who fought with the United Nations forces in Korea were greatly influenced by the hand and foot fighting techniques of their Korean counterparts. Many service personnel went a step further and initiated training in the arts themselves. The beautiful high kicks and devastating heel strikes were eagerly picked up by the GIs. They found that these unarmed combat methods far surpassed anything they had learned at boot camp.

When the war ended, the soldiers returned home, many of them taking taekwon-do black belt rankings with them.

Within 25 years, the American people adopted this ancient Korean system of combat to such an extent that out of all the martial arts practiced in the USA today, 60 percent of them are of Korean origin, or their derivatives. Many of the nation's top martial artists began their training in taekwon-do, including men such as Chuck Norris, who became the eight times undefeated champion of the world, and resident Korean instructors such as He Il Cho, who has instructed more students to world tournament level than perhaps anyone else.

The Art of Kicking

Taekwon-do's kicks have great destructive power, and utilize some unique techniques, although many other styles of martial arts employ similar kicks. But perfection cannot be achieved because other styles do not possess the knowledge of the important basic forms found only in taekwon-do. It is only when power, speed, and correct stance are blended that accuracy and maximum destructive force can be obtained.

His legs are the most powerful natural weapon that a human being possesses for the defense of his life. Taekwon-do bases its kicks on the bound-spring principle. Muscles and tendons, when subjected to excess tensile strain, lose their elastic power, much as a rubber band once overstretched, either snaps or loses its resilience. So the object in applying a kick is to be like a coiled spring that is suddenly released. Because so much emphasis is placed upon kicking in taekwon-do, a special series of stretching exercises was devised. These enable an exponent to train so that he may extend his legs to the standard required.

Martial Arts of the Orient

Previous pages, left *A taekwon-do adept leaps into a flying side kick over the backs of his fellow practitioners in order to break a suspended piece of wood. These kinds of power kicks are commonplace in taekwon-do.*

Previous pages, right *A spectacular demonstration of the double scissors kick executed at over ten feet in the air.*

Right *The son of the grandmaster of hwarang-do applies a high point kick front kick. The power behind one of these kicks can quite easily crush a man's nose with little difficulty.*

The Korean Tiger Division

In today's modern army in South Korea they have a special unit called the Tiger Division. All the soldiers in that division are practicing martial artists. No one may gain entry to this elite group unless he holds a black belt ranking, First Dan or better. It would seem that history has gone full circle, and the Koreans are back to the days of the Hwarang-Do.

Hapkido

There is one system of Korean martial art that exists solely and strictly for self-defense, and that is hapkido.

Although this art is related to tae kyon, where it gets its kicks and punches from, hapkido was formed with the marrying of aikido and tae kyon. In a self-defense situation, a hapkido practitioner would stand his ground and wait for the assault. As soon as the would-be attacker made his move a soft circular block would deflect the approaching blow. Then in a dazzling series of counter-offensive techniques involving spinning kicks, back kicks, and roundhouse kicks, the hapkidoist would pound his attacker into the ground. So effective is this art that, during the conflict in Vietnam, United States Green Berets were taught the skills of hapkido.

Hapkido Principles

The main difference between aikido and hapkido lies in the redirecting of the attacker. The hapkido man counterattacks so strongly and swiftly with tremendous force that the punishing onslaught totally overwhelms his adversary. Whereas in aikido, the main principle is just to quell the attack, without due force. A hapkido man will never meet an attack head on. Instead, he will step to the side and deflect the blow before going in with a murderous counterattack, taking maximum advantage of his opponent's motion.

Hapkido has more than 300 different major techniques in its system. And the permutations allow for a range of tens of thousands possible responses.

Pure Self-Defense

Because hapkido is primarily for self-defense purposes, it does not cater for patterns, forms, or *katas*, those imaginary shadow-boxing-type exercises seen in the other martial arts.

Extensive knowledge of pressure points and the body's vital areas are also scrupulously learnt, the sole concept being to avoid being harmed while trying to inflict as much damage as possible on the adversary.

Similarities in the kicking techniques of hapkido can be identified time and time again with taekwon-do. Because strength is not a critical factor in the art, hapkido lends itself to people of all ages and both sexes. In recent years many women, especially in the Santa Monica area of Los Angeles, have adopted hapkido to protect themselves.

One of the world's foremost authorities on this art is Korean-born Bong Soo Han, who resides in California.

The Hapkido symbol is written the same way as aikido, but the Korean pronunciation turns it into hapkido.

The art also places much emphasis on breaking techniques.

Tang Soo Do

Another Korean martial art that is enjoying great popularity in America is tang soo do, which means 'Way of the Tang Hand' when it originated, more than 2000 years ago it was known as soo bahk.

The present grandmaster of the art is Hwang Kee, who founded the world headquarters for tang soo do in Korea shortly after World War Two. The academy is known as the Moo Duk Kwan, and claims 20,000 member black belts world wide. Although tang soo do at first sight looks very similar to Japanese or Okinawan karate, this according to Hwang Kee, is because of the common Chinese ancestry of both arts.

The training hall where participants engage in their art is called a *dojang*. The training tunic or uniform is a *tobok*.

Hwarang-Do Arrives in America

The ancient warrior skills of hwarang-do arrived in the United States from Korea in 1972. Two brothers from Seoul, Joo Bang and Joo Sang Lee, set up a school to spread the system. The world headquarters for hwarang-do is in Downey, California. There, students learn the four basic sections within the art. They are, the internal power, external power, weapon power, and mental power. The system has 365 kicks, one for every day of the year.

Clairvoyance

Because of hwarang-do's emphasis on mental power, advanced students receive instruction in mind control. This leads to the development of ESP and clairvoyance with the ultimate aim of acquiring a sixth sense. Even the subject of telepathy is studied in great detail. The student of hwarang-do learns to become one with the laws of the universe. He believes that these powers, and more, lie within the potential of every human being and can be developed through the proper training methods.

Kill or Cure

In order to achieve a balance, hwarang-do practitioners learn medicine and healing in great detail. They believe that anyone who has the capability of causing injury and death to another human being should also possess the facility to heal as well. In effect, an adept of the art can kill or cure. Students learn a special type of finger pressure technique similar to acupressure. By manipulating certain points of the human anatomy, a practitioner can revive and cure a sick person or, for that matter, a vanquished mugger. This method is known as Royal Family Finger Healing.

Hwarang-Do Comes into the Open

Joo Bang Lee is the present grandmaster of the hwarang-do system. This title was accorded to him on the death of his own teacher, Suahm Dosa, in 1969. Joo Bang Lee became the 58th holder of the title, which has an unbroken lineage of 1,800 years. The Lee Brothers learnt their art in a Buddhist temple high in the mountains of Korea. After graduating in the system, they received permission to open up a school themselves.

This was the first time in modern history that hwarang-do had been taught outside the Buddhist monastery. The strict veils of secrecy had been swept aside, and the art was open to all those who wished to learn it.

The Sul Sa

The Sul Sa was a secret sect within the confines of hwarang-do. In ancient times its members were regarded as being almost magical because of the very special feats they performed. These special agents, or spies, underwent the most severe martial arts training possible. A Sul Sa could be classed almost as a one-man army. The job of the Sul Sa was to spy on the opposing forces, or assassinate the top enemy generals. It was said of them, that they could dislocate their own joints at will, to slip out of the most complicated knots.

Two fighters go into the attack at a national taekwon-do tournament. As karate has turned to competitive sport so, too, has taekwon-do.

It is hoped that taekwon-do will be the next martial art to gain entry to the Olympic Games in 1988.

They could scale the sheerest castle walls with ease, and actually walk on water using special boat-like shoes. Because of their techniques in camouflage it was thought that the Sul Sa could even make themselves invisible. All these things, combined with supreme empty hand and weapons techniques, made them invaluable to the forces of the Hwarang.

Modern Day Sul Sa

Today, many of the secret skills of the Sul Sa are being taught in America. One of the foremost authorities on the subject was the late Michael Enchanis, who learnt the art from his mentor, Joo Bang Lee. Enchanis, after his experiences in the Vietnam War with the 75th Ranger Battalion, began to wish for a martial art that could be geared for every encounter, no matter what it might be. He felt that although he had been given the best military training at the time, the American special forces still had a lot to learn about jungle and guerrilla warfare.

Training Begins

Using the knowledge gained in the study of hwarang-do from Joo Bang Lee, Michael Enchanis developed a brand new concept of training that would allow soldiers and special service personnel to cope with any situation. After convincing military chiefs at the Pentagon as to the effectiveness of the ancient Sul Sa methods adapted for modern warfare, he was given the go-ahead to teach selected men for a three-week training program. The course was conducted at Fort Bragg, North Carolina.

There, they learnt special unarmed combat methods, based upon the skills of hwarang-do. Included in the course was sentry stalking; defense against armed attack; mind control of the enemy, using advanced techniques of psychology; choking and neck-breaking; acupressure for self-healing; hypnosis for combat; and wilderness survival.

Enchanis devised special short cuts in training to enable him to succeed. Of the original 25 men, only 10 completed the gruelling course.

Thought and Mind Control

One of the most important aspects of modern Sul Sa training is teaching men to control their own thoughts as well as the thoughts of others. Meditation and some principles of Zen Buddhism are used. This is combined with an absolute positive attitude and the will to succeed. Controlling the thoughts of others is done by subtly using the power of suggestion and learning to talk in a relaxed manner, although there is deadly intent in the mind of the user.

The training experiment was a great success, and many thousands of American servicemen have since followed it.

Unfortunately Michael Enchanis, the instigator of this blending of ancient martial arts skills with modern day warfare, was killed in Nicaragua in a helicopter accident. But the skills he taught live on, and perhaps through these special techniques of blending the old with the new, many American lives will be saved to carry on the fight against terrorism and guerrilla warfare.

Above and right The tremendous versatility of Korean masters in powerbreaking demonstrations.
Opposite Great control is needed in a flying sidekick to the throat.

Other Forms of Japanese
Martial Arts

It is no disgrace to lose, if one has sought to win.

Left *A kyudo practitioner in full splendid regalia at a Japanese samurai festival. The lacquered armor is hand made and worth many thousands of dollars.*

Right *A Sumo wrestler decked out and ready to fight at the biggest event in the calendar, the sumo grand championship.*

The field of Japanese martial arts covers many interesting subjects. In the popularity stakes, judo and karate are the front runners, but there is a multitude of lesser known arts that are practiced with the same fervor and dedication. In times gone by, some of these martial arts were actual battlefield skills. Today in an age of push-button technology, they have been relegated to the status of hobbies or pastimes. But a few are alive and very much as deadly as they were 500 years ago. They are practiced by a few devoted traditionalists whose aim is to keep alive the skills of their ancestors.

Sumo — The Indigenous Art of Japan
Nowhere else in the world can be found an art quite like sumo. It is strictly an indigenous art or sport belonging to Japan and consists of two huge man mountains trying to push each other out of a wrestling ring.

Sumo wrestlers compete on a dirt mound called a *dohyo,*

which is 15 feet in diameter. A contestant loses immediately if any part of his body, other than the soles of his feet, scrapes or lands on the surface of the dohyo.

The Blink of an Eye
The whole subject of sumo wrestling is steeped in Shintoism, Shinto being one of the religions of Japan. Because of the nature of the contest, a match only lasts a few seconds — it's all over in the blink of an eye.

There is much ceremony and formality, which to Western eyes seems endless. There are 48 classical throws that can end a sumo match, and contests that last longer than a minute are extremely rare. A sumo wrestler has no right of protest, the decision of the referee being final. There are no tied matches, and in the case of a close contest when it has been difficult to determine the winner, a re-match is ordered. Sumo is the only body contact sport in which there are no weight groups.

Left *Novices going through limbering up exercises at a sumo training class in Japan.*

Below *In a ceremony of purification, a sumo wrestler scoops up salt from the floor in order to throw it around the ring.*

Sumo History

Japanese legend tells of the first ever sumo match, which was supposedly held when the god Takemikazuchi won a bout with the leader of a rival tribe. The first matches were a form of ritual dedicated to the gods. In those days it was known as *sumai,* and fights were often fought to the death. Fighters wear a silk loin cloth called a *mawashi,* which is 10 yards long and 2 feet wide. It is folded, then wrapped around the waist of the wrestler. A fighter begins each contest by stamping his feet. This is to drive away all the evil spirits from the ring (sumo men are very superstitious). They also extend their hands to indicate that they bear no concealed weapons.

When Commodore Matthew Perry arrived in Japan in his 'black ships', the authorities made certain that on the shore to greet him were the top sumo men of the day. This was to show the unwelcome Americans that they should not underestimate the size of the Japanese people.

Modern Sumo Matches

Today in Japan, sumo is both a professional and an amateur sport. A series of 15 day tournaments are held six times a year. All matches begin from a crouch position. Before a bout takes place there is a lengthy pre-fight ritual. At one point the wrestler grabs a handful of salt and tosses it into the ring as an act of purification. Unless he is familiar with the traditions of the Shinto religion, many of these pre-fight rituals are completely meaningless to the visiting Westerner. Hundreds of years ago women participated in the matches, but these days all that has been banned.

The American Sumo Champion

As already stated, sumo is strictly indigenous to Japan. But one Westerner broke through the barriers of its thousand-year-old tradition to become a sumo champion. Hawaiian-born Jesse Kahualua, became the first non-oriental to attain the highest level in the sport.

Left *Novice sumo wrestlers try out their first techniques in front of a huge crowd at an open air demonstration in Japan.*

Below *As a sumo grand champion prepares for his fight, an attendant offers the ritual salt bag for purification.*

Far left *Two massive sumo wrestlers clinch in the center of the ring. The first to be thrown out loses the contest.*

Left, above *The Yokozuna class of grand champions at a shinto shrine open up the sumo season for wrestling. The sport draws huge and enthusiastic audiences throughout Japan.*

Left, below *The bout begins and with awsome power the two wrestlers attempt to push one another outside the circle.*

Right *Novice sumo wrestlers grapple with each other, much to the delight of the knowledgeable crowd that has turned out to see how these beginners shape up.*

Feats of Strength

The prime requisite in sumo wrestling is strength. The hips are the center of balance and leverage for the sumo man. When this balance is combined with bodyweight, flexibility, speed and strength, the sumo wrestler is virtually immovable. Strange as it may seem, a sumo wrestler can do a complete side split until he sits, flat on the ground, even though he carries a weight of more than 350 pounds. Stories are told of a sumo wrestler who stood in front of an army jeep, braced himself, and told the driver to accelerate. Although the tires churned away furiously and the smell of burning rubber filled the air, the giant wrestler stood his ground as solid as a rock, and the jeep could not move. Sometimes, the wrestlers will invite five or six men from the audience to have a go at trying to push them over, and the volunteers seldom succeed.

Unwritten Laws of Sumo Wrestling

Although the rules in a Sumo match are relatively few, there is a certain sumo code that is strictly adhered to. In the *Yokozuna* (grand champion) class, the wrestler must be able continually to demonstrate his superiority. If a grand champion loses more than eight bouts in a tournament he will voluntarily retire. This is the unspoken rule of all Yokozunas.

The sumo wrestler's topknot is not applied until the wrestler reaches the makuuchi division. Then his hair will not be cut until he retires from sumo.

The sumo wrestler's ritual of scattering salt in the ring before the fight must take at least four minutes. He is judged by the audience as to how he performs this rite. It is up to each novice sumo wrestler to take responsibility for his own eating habits.

Kyudo — The Way of the Bow

Archery played a major part in ancient Japanese warfare, and the art of *kyujutsu* was developed as a means of perfecting combat techniques with bow and arrow, when peace finally settled on Japan the jutsu arts became do arts. *Jutsu* referred to feudal combative skills, where the aim was to kill. A *do* form is a road, path, or way. It is a means to a way or method of promoting self-understanding and perfection through martial skills.

Thus the kyujutsu of the battlefield became the kyudo of today, although the ancient rituals and ceremony involved in the art have never altered.

Kyudo Doctrine

Linked very closely to the study of Zen, kyudo is a highly formalized martial art in which the ultimate aim for the archer is to compete and overcome himself. With proper concentration, man and bow fuse together until they are one. Then and only then, at the right instant, will the arrow be automatically released. Kyudo is not all about hitting the bullseye, or for that matter even the target. The important point is how the shooting is done, and the archer's state of mind when the arrow is released. Kyudo of Japan is a combination of the physical art with the philosophical principles of Zen Buddhism. There is perhaps more emphasis placed on the Zen concept, in Japanese archery, that in all the other martial arts save maybe for kendo.

The Bow and Arrow

Unlike its European counterpart, the kyudo bow is an unusual size and shape. It is more than six feet long and is constructed entirely of bamboo, fashioned to the same traditional design of the Samurai who originally used it so well. It has a weight pull of around 80 pounds. The bow grip is not centered, like the old English longbow, but is placed approximately one-third of the distance from the bottom of the bow. The kyudo bow is the longest in the world. The length of the arrows ranges from three feet to three-and-a-half feet. The bowstring is made from hemp. A quiver is never used in kyudo, the archer preferring to hold a second arrow in his bowstring hand.

Robin Hood of Japan

Just as England had its Robin Hood and Switzerland its William Tell, Japan had its great archer hero, named Nasu no Yoichi. In 1280, when the warlike clans of Japan were struggling for supremacy, two great clans met in what was to be a decisive battle. It occurred along the coast of Japan's Inland Sea, at a place called Yashima. One of the clans, the Genji, had managed to drive the enemy forces into the sea.

Previous pages, left *A lady archer raises her bow, whilst her eyes remain on the target. In kyudo the aim is not important; the emphasis is more on the state of the mind.*

Previous pages, right *A modern-day samurai wearing the apparel of the traditionaly mounted kyudo bowman. He is taking part in the Soma annual festival. The tips of the arrows have different points, for specific jobs.*

Left *Two kyudo — an infantry bowman and a mounted bowman. The mounted bowman does not wear the restrictive legging armor.*

From the bridge of the enemy ship the enemy lord, belonging to the Heike clan, hoisted a beautiful golden fan with the royal crest upon it. The fan flickered from the mast in the wind. The Heike lord laughingly challenged the Genji Samurai on the beach to shoot it down. Nasu no Yoichi accepted the challenge. Taking careful aim, he focused on the barely visible target that was bobbing and fluttering with the movement of the ship. After what seemed like minutes, Nasu released his arrow. It sailed across the beach, over the waves for nearly 400 yards (so legend says), and suddenly found its mark in the center pin where the fine ribs of the fan were held together. The golden fan split into pieces and dropped into the sea. The Heike soldiers were completely dismayed at this bad omen. The Samurai of the Genji clan, after witnessing such an incredible feat of marksmanship, renewed their attack and the Heike clan were crushed completely.

Kyudo Today

Kyudo is practiced by more than half a million Japanese today. It is a great favorite with women because it is thought to enhance grace and manners.

Those who embrace the art of kyudo as their way of enlightenment must be prepared for years of training. Traditionally, a student will be taught to breathe properly, how to relax, how to adopt the correct posture, how to let his mind take over. All this is learned for nearly 18 months, before he is ever allowed to shoot his first arrow. Although much has been said of the Zen concept in kyudo, in a lighter vein it is also a practical sport. Competitors do their best to score a bull. This side to kyudo resembles Western archery, but is frowned upon by the ardent traditionalists.

The Naginata — Women's Weapon of Self-Defense

Naginata, to all intents and purposes, is a female sport. The naginata is a type of halberd that foot soldiers used on the battlefields of Japan more than 500 years ago.

In recent times, it has become a popular sport among the women of Japan. It is even taught in girls' high schools up and down the country. Today the live blade has been replaced by an angled piece of plaited bamboo. In wielding the naginata, the motions are circular and flowing, not sharp and straight. This makes for flexibility and suppleness, and helps tone up the body. Naginata takes much less strength to practice than kendo, hence its overwhelming popularity with women.

The Battlefield Weapon

The art of the naginata dates back to when foot soldiers used to mount short swords on poles. This enabled them to take a swipe at the legs of horses in an effort to unseat their riders. Eventually the naginata became a standard weapon in warfare. When the wars ceased, a shortened version of the weapon was kept in every Samurai's home. This was intended for use by the women of the house should she be attacked or burglarised while the master was out in the service of his lord. Japanese homes being small and low-ceilinged, it was not easy for the occupant to wield a large weapon. So the shortened naginata was introduced for use by women.

Naginata Equipment

In the practice of naginata-do, to give it the correct term, the old standard six-and-a-half-foot weapon is used. Each end is covered with a leather tip. A face mask, the same as that used in kendo (called a *men*), is employed by the ladies for protection. This, combined with a special breastplate, arm and shin guards, and a girdle of protective padding, completes the uniform.

The sport form of naginata-do has mushroomed since introduction of tournament competition in the 1960s.

Previous pages, left *Because of the zen aspects of kyudo, many women in Japan have adopted this ancient art.*

Previous pages, right *The aim matters the least in kyudo, and it is not unusual to find masters of the art actually firing the bow with their eyes shut. The quality of the act takes precedence over everything else.*

Left *The Japanese short spear was kept in most samurai's homes before the advent of the naginata. The yari, as it was known, fell into disuse when the naginata became popular.*

Above *Two combatants give battle wielding the traditional weapons of feudal Japan — the samurai sword and the naginata. Both are wearing the hakama or split skirt, the standard uniform in today's naginata schools.*

Right *Three competitors line up ready to take part in the modern sporting form of naginata-do. The armoured breastplate and headmask are compulsory, so as to prevent injury to the fighters. The naginata has been replaced with a bamboo replica.*

Iai-Do, the Skill of the Quick Draw Sword

Iai-do is the art of the quick draw, using a *katana* or Samurai sword. It was developed into a do form from the old skill of iaijutsu, in which the Samurai would draw his sword upon a sudden encounter, and slay the enemy who had tried to ambush him. It can be likened to the technique of the old fast-draw gunfighters in Western movies. A man named Hayashizaki Jinsuke formulated this quick-draw style in the mid-16th century. As a result, he founded the famous schools of Muso Shinden Ryu.

Left *The white-garbed figure of an Iai-do disciple going through his routine of the quick draw sword and the sheathing of it. Iai-do instils discipline and self-cultivation in its adepts.*

Modern Martial Discipline

Today, Iai-do is a form of martial training that is practiced alone. Once a student has received the correct tuition, the rate of improvement depends entirely upon himself. Much ceremony is accorded to the placing of the sheathed sword into the belt or *obi*. There is a certain aspect of Zen in this procedure. Constant practice and understanding of the traditions behind the art is needed before an adept is ready to try out the fast draw. In the past, Western students who tried to rush the training and mental discipline often regretted it, because in doing so they severed their fingers and in some cases the whole of the hand on the razor-sharp edge of the sword blade. Iai-do is a noncombative art.

Above *Two Kaseda samurai practice with the ancient war weapons of feudal Japan. Part of the annual samurai festival of Kyushu Japan.*

Right *An enthraled audience watches with fascination at a samurai descendant as he demonstrates the power of his weapon slicing through an oak pole.*

Martial Arts of the Orient

Shorinji Kempo

Shorinji kempo is a martial art that developed 1000 years ago at Shaolin in China. One may think for that reason that it is a kung fu system, but it is not. Shorinji kempo is the Japanese reading of Shaolin fist. The whole system was rinsed through, with techniques being added, others being dropped and restyled, to become known as Shorinji kempo. It was devised by Michiomi Nakano, who later became known as Doshin So. It began life, in the modern context, just after World War Two, in Japan. The system has at the core, a form of Buddhism known as Kongo Zen. The philosophy embraced within this system encourages self-help, and teaches that man's individual progress through life is dependent on his own efforts. Although the art claims Chinese ancestry, many of its movements resemble jiu jitsu and aiki-jitsu. The principles of shorinji place equal emphasis on the use of both soft and hard techniques.

The Black Dragon Society

The founder of shorinji, Doshin So, spent much of his life in Manchuria under the patronage of Mitsuru Toyama, the founder of the secret society known as the Black Dragon. This was an organization to promote political unrest in Asia. In his twenties Doshin So was sent to China to spy for the Japanese government. While he was there he visited the old Shaolin temple, and at once was greatly impressed with the martial techniques of the monks. He began to practice martial arts eagerly, and after further travels around China he met many masters of almost extinct systems of kempo and kung fu, and trained with them.

After the war, Doshin So returned to Japan and brought his form of martial art out into the open. He had completely revised, and expanded the original system.

Today there are more than 800 training halls around Japan for shorinji kempo with 300,000 member students. Although Doshin So died quite recently, the headmastership was taken over by his daughter who is the sole leader of shorinji kempo around the world.

The aim of the pursuit of kempo is the Dharma spirit.

Previous pages Modern exponents practicing ancient martial skills, at the Kaseda Samurai festival in Kyushu, Japan.

Right Two exponents of Shorinji kempo in traditional fighting garb demonstrating the power in the throw and the ease with which it is facilitated. The technique is all in the action of the wrist. The defender flows into the movement smoothly using the attacker's energy to aid him in his throw.

Kendo

Kendo, just like Iai-do and naginata-do, are severe traditional martial arts that offer their students something that goes far deeper than mere competitive sport. This aspect of the traditional values is probably the underlying motivation that brings most novices into kendo. It is for this reason that kendo instructors remind new students that they must never forget that they are joining a society that tries to follow a very ancient training whose rigors they accept for the moral values that lie behind them.

The Way of the Sword

Traditionally the sword represented the Samurai warrior's soul. For someone other than the owner to touch it without permission, even inadvertently, represented a great insult and was often punished by death if the offender was a peasant. If another Samurai offended, it could lead to a duel. *Kendo* means 'the Way of the Sword'. Unlike Western swordplay, Japanese sword fighting consisted of a series of complicated cuts, or sometimes just one downward slash, to gain victory over an opponent.

Left *A young kendoka attends to the important task of securing his face mask before taking part in competition. As with everything in kendo, even the donning of the uniform is performed ceremonially.*

Right *A typical kendo class in Japan. The youngsters prepare themselves for daily practice by first calming their minds and inner feelings.*

Left *All geared and ready to fight, students listen attentively to their sensei instructing them in dojo behavior.*

Above, left to right *Two kendo competitors fight each other with all the fury the sport demands. Their shinai or bamboo swords clack with a crash and their heels leave the floor as each attempts to come down with force upon his opponent's head with the shinai.*

Right *Young kendokas in action during a typical tournament fight. The intensity with which combatants fight each other can be quite startling; yet at the end of a match they are still the best of friends.*

Modern Kendo

Early Japanese fencing schools sought to teach effective techniques to train their warriors, without actually using a real blade because mistakes with a real sword during training proved to be quite costly in terms of human life. So the heavy oak *bokken* was invented. This consisted of a piece of hard red oak with the shape, weight, and balance of a real sword. But this, too, caused injuries, some of them fatal. In an attempt to further reduce the injury level, a bamboo sword called a *shinai* was devised. This was made of four pieces of bamboo shaped and fitted together by fiber and encased in animal skin. This shinai is the weapon used in today's modern competition fighting.

Kendo Armor

Kendoka (those who practice kendo), when training or fighting in competition, wear protective armor called *bogu*. This consists of a heavy steel helmet called a *men*, which weighs around six or seven pounds. A breastplate called the *do* and gauntlet-type gloves named *kote* are the basic protection used, together with *tare*, a lower waist protector.

All kendo armor is tremendously expensive, even a cheap outfit being likely to cost upwards of 500 dollars. The traditional split skirt or *hakama*, completes the kendo fighter's attire.

Basic Movements

Training for kendo requires much physical stamina because the fighter must be able to bear the smashing blows of the shinai. He has to move around with agility, weighed down by all the body armor, and still wield his own weapon at an opponent. Kendo, like any other Oriental fighting discipline, has basic moves which, when used in sequence, become intricate maneuvers. One particular movement, called *chiburi*, is where an exponent has imagined he has killed somebody with a sword cut. He has to execute a downward flick with the blade to shake off the victim's blood before returning the sword to the scabbard.

The Master Swordsman

The most renowned swordsman in all Japan was the Samurai named Miyamoto Musashi, sometimes called *Kensei*, or sword saint. Born in 1584, Musashi was completely devoted to kendo, and by the age of 30 had fought and won more than 60 contests, killing all his opponents. Musashi pursued the ideal of the warrior searching for enlightenment along the perilous paths of kendo and duelling. Life for him was a series of challenges and obstacles to be overcome.

He was convinced he was invincible, and to all intents and purposes he probably was. He retired to the mountains, during his last years, to formulate a principle of philosophy and strategy. This he wrote down and called *Go Rin No Sho* or *A Book of Five Rings*. This masterpiece, as it has been called, is today used by Japanese businessmen as a guide to the strategy of pulling off multi-million dollar deals. Musashi died in 1645. When near to death, he wrote 'When you have attained the way of strategy there will not be one thing that you cannot understand'.

The Essence of Kendo

It is difficult for the average person to understand the essence of kendo. Its main purpose is not the acquisition of technique but instead directed towards the improvement of spirit and one's moral conduct. All true swordsmen carried with them the concept that technical skill and the development of the spiritual man were inseparable. Even today many kendoka believe that to practice kendo purely as a sport is to pervert its essential purpose.

In 1971 the International Kendo Federation was formed to unite the eight million or so kendo devotees around the world into one body.

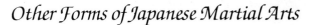

Previous pages *A Japanese kendo children's class. The popularity of this sport — culled from the ancient warrior ways — has grown to quite epic proportions worldwide.*

Above and right *Two kendoka — members of the Emperor's Guard at the Imperial Palace, Tokyo — engage each other for their daily practice. In the background the referee watches diligently. Kendo is practiced every day by the Imperial Guard who are versed in several different martial arts to blackbelt standard. Because of their rank as Imperial Guards they are expected to be above average in kendo. This is the legacy handed down to them from their sword-wielding forefathers, when efficiency with a blade made the difference between life and death.*

The Ninja Clans of Death

Ninjutsu means 'stealth art' or 'stealing in'. Its practitioners are called *ninja*. It is said to originate from a Chinese military tactic and guerilla warfare book called *The Art of War*, written in the 4th century by a Chinese general named Sun Tsu. It is assumed that Japanese scholars had read the book during their culture-gathering journeys to China. From these seeds grew the deadly clans that were to be feared throughout Japan for centuries. The most famous ninja clans were born and trained in the Iga and Koga areas of Japan's main island, Honshu. Unlike most espionage systems where recruits were drawn from the military or law enforcement services, the ninja were born into it, coming from what were known as ninja families.

The Foundation of Secrecy

Secrecy was the foundation of the ninja tradition and it was because of this that their training camps and strongholds were always located in remote mountainous regions. It was there that the young ninjas trained from the age of about five. There was no distinction between boys and girls — all had to learn the trade of death. The girls, as they grew older and their female attributes became more obvious, trained in a different way. They were taught the powers of seduction, but still retained the ultimate aim of silent killing. This dreaded secret society of espionage experts cum assassins, would strike fear into the boldest of Samurai hearts when known to be working in their particular area. The ninja would creep forth, spilling out of the shadows of the night dressed all in black, and strike his allotted target, which would be either a rich lord or a powerful and important Samurai. Then, with the deed done, he would blend back into the night like a phantom.

Far left *A ninja in full field dress. His sword is much shorter and straighter than the traditional samurai sword.*

Left *Stealth and surprise were the two main weapons of the ninja. A ninja would hide for days then at an opportune moment suddenly as if out of nowhere he would appear and pounce on his surprised victim. Stealth and surprise were the two main weapons of the ninja.*

Far left Confronted by a ninja the ethical samurai fought with honor, whilst the devious and tricky assassin of the night would resort to any tactic or weapon that would give him the kill and complete his mission.

Left The ninja's sword was usually made out of quite cheap materials and was regarded by him as just another tool of the trade. To the samurai his blade was everything: his honor, his very soul.

Below A modern-day exponent of ninjitsu, Stephen Hayes in a stance with a short wooden pole known as a hanbo. The ninja could fight with great efficiency with almost any weapon that came to hand. When out on a mission, the ninja was limited to only the weapons and supplies he could carry on his person.

Feared Throughout the Land

The ninja and their exploits of instant assassination became so talked about, that the peasants, most of whom were uneducated, began to believe that the ninja were ghosts sent from another world just to kill. Stories of ninja assassinations spread like wildfire from village to village and from town to town. And so, for 700 years or more, the mere mention of ninja would turn lord and peasant alike white with terror. Of course, for the ninja this was an ideal situation because fear is a very powerful weapon and worked well for them on many occasions. Stories abounded of how the ninja could walk on water, pass through solid walls, disappear at will, and even change themselves into some horrific demon. The tales were a blend of imagination running riot and greatly exaggerated facts. But for the ninja they worked.

Ninja Training Camps

A young ninja's training began with the basic martial arts. He was required to become proficient to master level with at least four weapons. Early training began with the five basic skills — balance, agility, strength, stamina, and special skills. It was these special skills that put the ninja in a class of his own. This unique and very specialized training had, for the most part, to begin at a very early age when the children's bones and ligaments were soft and pliable. After years of stretching and joint manipulation, a field ninja was capable of dislocating his joints at will. This was particularly useful if he was ever captured and bound. By dislocating certain joints, he could release himself and escape.

Breathing and meditation were also taught. Breath control was paramount for the ninja especially when escaping by water, where it was reputed that a ninja could hold his breath under the surface for as long as three minutes. Also, by means of shallow breathing, he could enter a room full of sleeping men and control his heartbeats so as not to give himself away. A ninja learnt all about woodcraft, tracking, and survival, and was also a competent herbalist, being conversant with the use of poisons and their antidotes.

The Master of Disguise

The ninja served all masters, anyone at all, without discrimination. Their services and skills were for hire to perform any dirty or dangerous task without question. It was not unknown for one ninja clan to be pitted against another. All ninja were accomplished actors and masters of disguise, for the ninja had many roles to play in the practice of his black art. His athletic abilities included being able to run 125 miles in one day and hang from a tree branch for hours at a time. He could climb great heights, swim long distances, and was extremely proficient in unarmed combat.

The Mission

Usually a ninja on a mission carried only what he could safely house upon his person. Shoulder packs or bags would only hamper his movement. But his special garb, that all-black uniform, had many concealed pockets in which he could hide the tools of his trade. These included such items as *shuriken*, the sharp pointed throwing star, often tipped with a deadly poison; dried food for his journey; rope; medicines; and a special claw device made from leather and iron that fitted around his wrists to enable him to climb and grip on hard surfaces such as castle walls. Castles in Japan were made of wood.

The ninja sword, which he usually wore slung over his back, was unlike the Samurai's traditional *katana*. It was much shorter in length and had a straighter blade. This gave him greater mobility when fighting in the low-ceilinged Japanese rooms of the feudal era. The scabbard was longer than it needed to be. This enabled the ninja to carry items in the detachable bottom of the scabbard.

Left Chain weapons were a particular favorite of the ninja, anything that could ensnare and tangle an adversary. Here a kusari gamma is being used to entrap the typical attack from a samurai sword.

Right Springing from behind a rock the ninja pounces on his victim and ensnares his weapon with a kyoketsu shoge or ninja hook knife. The cord strangles the victim or at least incapacitates him, whilst the hook knife, which is attached to the cord, kills him.

The Assassination

A ninja sent out to kill someone might have to wait hours, or even days, before his target came within reach. So all his special skills were needed to prevent his being discovered. In one old legend a ninja was sent out to kill a particular lord. The lord's castle was guarded day and night and virtually impossible to enter. But the ninja still gained entry. After he had sought out his victim, who not unnaturally had a retinue of bodyguards around him, the ninja worked out a plan for the lord's demise. The black-garbed assassin concealed himself under the lord's private toilet and waited for him to come to the only place where he could be sure the lord would be by himself. As the lord entered and performed his daily habit, the ninja pierced his body with a short spear and killed him outright. However fanciful that old story may be, it does at least exemplify the lengths to which a ninja would go to fulfill his task of assassination and murder.

The Ninja Hierarchy

The ninja hierarchy was built up in three tiers. The first were the *jonin*, usually the chiefs or bosses who were at the top of the tree. A step lower down were the *chunin*, the middle-ranking ninja, the go-betweens, the ones whom people approached and paid to get the dirty jobs done. The lowest rung of the ladder was made up of the *genin* or field ninja. They were the ones who carried out most of the work and took all the risks. All ninja took a blood oath of secrecy. If any of them broke this oath they were hunted down and killed mercilessly. If a field agent were ever captured by the enemy he could expect to be horribly tortured and put to death slowly. Because of this, a captured ninja was expected to commit suicide before he could be forced through torture to divulge who had hired him for his mission, or even worse, betray some of the clan's innermost secrets. Yet, knowing that all this could happen to him, the ninja still plied his deadly trade with supreme efficiency.

Left *Ninja poised with shuriken, one of the bladed throwing stars kept in a pouch pocket and used for throwing at sentries from a distance. The points of shuriken were usually tipped with poison.*

Right *A ninja uses every part of his highly trained body to trap his enemy. With one foot wedged against his attacker's sword blade, the ninja's hook knife is about to strike. The ninja (inset) surprises his enemy and tangles his weapon in a web of chain. Most ninja weapons were designed to be multi-purpose. Even the sword had several distinct uses.*

The Fighting Kingdom of
Siam

To know the outcome, look to the root.
Study the past to know the future.

Left *A Thai boxing master in his ring regalia.*

Right *A back heel kick going straight in at its target. Although the defender has tried to use the rising knee block to stop it, he applied it too late to count, and the devastating kick gets through to the target.*

Wherever one may wander in the Orient among the many schools of fighting arts one will not find a deadlier group of combatants than the kick boxers of Thailand. Many great masters in the martial arts accept that the Thai boxer is lethal because he is a professional and lives just to fight. Many people look upon *muay thai* (the correct term for Thai boxing) as a sport. This may be partly true, but the legacy of this 2000-year-old art lives on today in the hearts of the Thai people. One visit to Thailand will confirm this. Down any street one can see young children going through the rudiments of this ancient Siamese fighting art.

Muay Thai's Early Rise
The old Kingdom of Siam, as Thailand was once known, has from ancient times always seen trouble from its neighbors. Occupying the Southeast Asia peninsula, it has Burma on the west, Laos on the north and east, Cambodia to the southeast, and the Gulf of Siam and Malaysia on the south. Yet amazingly this 'Land of the Free' has resisted all

attempts to conquer it. One can only put this down to the fierce fighting spirit of the people. Muay thai techniques were part of the military training system, which was greatly influenced by Chinese fighting methods in the beginning. It later underwent a marked change and developed independently, losing many of the Chinese boxing methods along the way. It is somewhat of a mystery how and why this happened, and for that matter why many of muay thai's special fighting techniques are not seen anywhere else outside Thailand.

The Tiger King
Because the Siamese people were combative by nature, the common folk picked up the military unarmed fighting methods and developed them into a sport, but they still retained all the lethal blows. Further skills were developed during the reign of King Pra Chao Sua, who was known as the Tiger King. Every village staged its prize fights, with young and old, rich and poor all taking part. The king

himself was a highly skilled boxer and was reputed to have trained with his soldiers six hours a day. He would often leave his palace disguised as a wandering peasant and enter boxing events, always defeating the local champions. The king would spend hours alone in his palace perfecting certain techniques, and then try them out in local contests. So skilled were some of his boxing strategies that even today they are still used and known as the Tiger King style.

The Greatest Fighter of Them All

Over the centuries the greatest of the muay thai fighters have become legendary. Stories are told of their battles and adventures to eager listening children by the village storyteller. Perhaps the most famous of all Siamese fighters was Nai Khanom Dtom. He was a brilliant athlete and a strong courageous man, holding the title of the best fighter in all Siam. During the many wars that Siam had with her neighbor Burma, Nai Khanom Dtom was captured by Burmese soldiers. They had heard of his great fighting ability so they decided to pit him against 12 of Burma's top bando fighters (*Bando* is the martial art of Burma, and similar to Thai boxing), and if he could defeat all 12, Nai

Khanom Dtom would be allowed to go free.

So the next day in a stadium packed with thousands of people, Nai Khanom Dtom prepared to fight bare-handed against the cream of Burma's best fighters. One by one they came at him, all out to kill him and become heroes themselves for defeating the greatest martial artist in Siam. As each fighter pitted his skills against the great Nai Khanom Dtom, he was instantly killed, being dispatched with lightning elbow strikes and murderous knee blows. As the day wore on, the great Siamese champion had slain nine of his adversaries. The spectators, who had been cheering for their own men, suddenly began to cheer for this magnificent fighter from Siam. They were full of admiration for the prisoner who had fought and killed nine men without rest or being wounded himself. By the end of the day 12 bodies lay in the dry dust of the stadium, and standing tall and undefeated was the great Nai Khanom Dtom. The King of Burma had no alternative but to let him go free.

Today, many centuries after that event, Thai boxers honor him by dedicating one fight night each year to Nai Khanom Dtom.

Left The official regalia from the Thai arsenal: the krabi-krabong sword, the boxing gloves and the monkon.

Right A Thai boxer performs the ritual pre-fight dance called ram muay.

Following pages, right The sok or elbow is one of the most lethal weapons the Thai boxer uses and the technique when correctly applied can cause death. In Western Thai boxing tournaments the blow has been outlawed.

Following pages, left A Thai boxer executes a superb high point roundhouse kick.

No Rules or Regulations

In 1930 muay thai underwent a transformation. A number of rules and regulations were introduced including the wearing of boxing gloves and groin guards, and certain weight divisions were stipulated. Until that time, virtually anything was allowed in the ring. One favorite device used by the boxers was hemp rope bound around the fist to act as a form of glove. Then it was dipped in glue and rolled in finely ground glass. The effects of this adjunct in the ring were dramatic.

Deaths in the Ring

The elbow and the knee are probably the Thai boxer's deadliest weapons. It was because of uncontrolled elbow blows to the head, especially the temple, that most of the deaths occurred in the ring during fights. The knee attacks to the groin left many fighters with smashed testicles. Muay thai was known as a tough art. In order to survive at all, a fighter had to be quicker and stronger and more skilled than his opponent. Even in the small mountain villages deaths in the ring were common, right up until World War Two. But new rules quickly put an end to the staggering death toll in the ring.

Growth of the Art Today

With the spread of contact sport among martial artists throughout the world, Thai boxing has burgeoned all over Asia. In Japan, Thai boxing has reached epic proportions in recent years. Nowadays the deadly elbow strike is banned, except in Thailand. Followers of many other martial disciplines will on most occasions refuse to fight a Thai boxer because they regard him as a complete fighting machine honed to proficiency through years of hard and intensive training. Those who dare to take up the challenge usually taste bitter defeat.

Training a Thai Boxer

As soon as a little Thai boy can walk he is introduced to kick boxing. Virtually 95 percent of all Thai youngsters begin boxing in earnest before they even learn how to read and write. Every village, town, and city has some form of boxing ring or stadium. If a youth shows any kind of promise in competition he is sent to one of the many special training camps scattered around the country. There the youngsters will eat, sleep, and live Thai boxing. The training regimen is very strict and life is hard, but a successful fighter can earn a lot of money during his time in the ring.

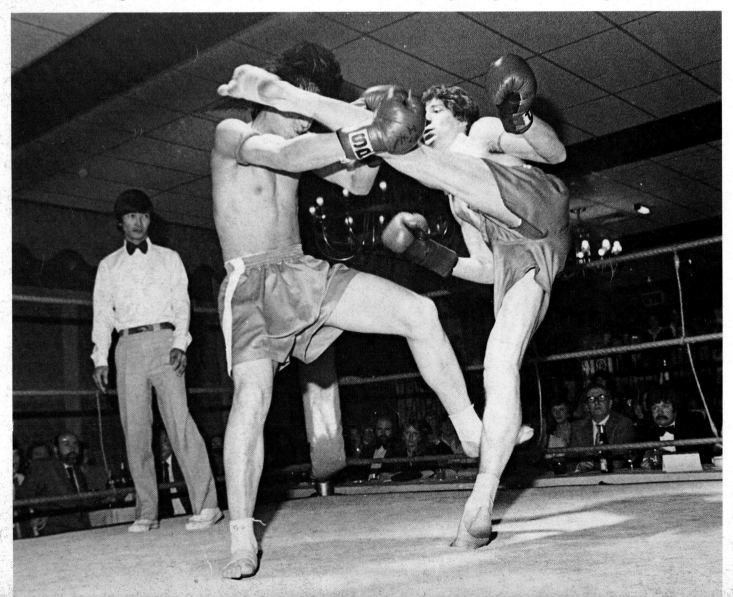

Stamina

In the training of a boxer, much emphasis is placed upon stamina, for it is this energy that keeps a man moving fast enough and long enough to win the fight. To build up this stamina much roadwork is done. At the *prakong* (training camp) fighters run up to 10 miles a day. After a short rest, they plunge into the river and swim, forever building up endurance. From there they go onto the bags, and spend hours kicking away until their legs feel like lead. Then they undergo a unique series of stretching exercises. It is all this severe and intensive training that makes Thai boxers what they are. Because young fighters work so hard and tend to lead an austere and frugal existence, there is little danger of their gaining weight or getting fat in the wrong places. Most champion muay thai fighters look thin and undernourished, but underneath that exterior beats the heart of a lion with the strength and vitality to match

Good Luck Charms and Superstitions

As with many combatants through the ages, Western or Eastern, the wearing of talismans, or the use of charms, spells, and good luck pieces plays an important part in the gladiatorial make-up of a Thai boxer. They use these talismans for protection in the ring. They have an unshakable conviction that such items can transform them into invulnerable supermen. Muay thai fighters have a multitude of such amulets. Their faith is partly superstitious and partly religious. One superstition concerns the use of the *nan* leaf (pronounced 'whan'). A

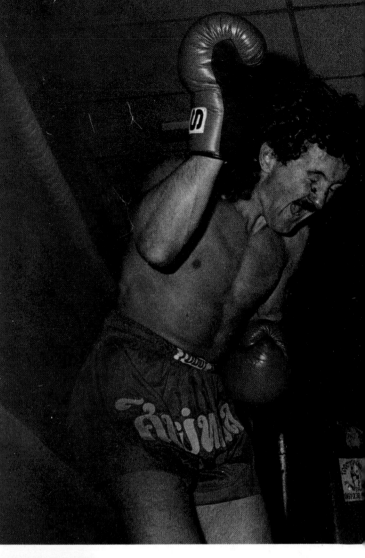

Above *A Thai boxing contestant in agony after receiving a full punch body blow to the stomach.*

Left *At the climax of a tournament two Thai boxers slug it out.*

Right *A Thai boxer demonstrates the finer points of the ritual ram muay dance.*

fighter puts this leaf in his mouth before a fight, usually under the tongue, in the belief that by doing so he gains protection against elbow and knee attacks. He believes that the leaf somehow makes his skin thick and, as a result he will not bleed or even get cut.

The Guardian Spirit

Another good luck ritual exercised by the fighters when entering the ring, is to place offerings in the form of flowers to the guardian spirit of the ring, to grant them victory over their opponent. The fighters also wear a cord called *kruang rang* tied around their upper arm. This usually conceals a miniature statue or figure of the lord Buddha. Other superstitions forbid women to enter the ring. Their presence allegedly radiates bad vibrations and brings bad luck to the fighters. But since the establishment of women's Thai boxing leagues in recent years, this particular belief is now aimed only at females who are not fighters.

The Religious Aspect of Muay Thai

Perhaps we in the West are not yet fully aware of the important way in which religion and the martial arts go hand in hand in the East. This dualism seems to be something of a contradiction in Western terms but it is no accident that the scientific principles of combat were, more often than not, formulated in monasteries and temples. Muay thai practitioners are devoutly religious, and their art is firmly rooted in Therevada Buddhism. In fact, many young fighters have served time as disciples in monasteries before going to the boxing camps.

Ram Muay — the Deadly Dance

Before any fighter begins a fight, he goes through a ritualistic dance known as *ram muay,* or pre-fight dance. Every camp has its own form of this dance, and to the seasoned spectator it is quite possible to tell which camp the fighter has come from without knowing anything about him. The pre-fight ritual of ram muay also serves to tone up the fighter's muscles. Interestingly enough, within the dance lie all the basic moves of Thai boxing.

The boxing masters have their own ideas as to how this dance should be performed. When the fighter emerges from his corner to begin his ram muay it indicates to all present that he is showing great respect to the master who taught him his art. This little gesture of obeisance to the teacher is called *wai kruh.*

The Dance Begins

The fighter begins by bowing three times in the direction of the camp he came from. This acknowledges the camp, his parents, and Buddha. The whole idea of the ritual is to try and psyche out his opponent and instil fear into him, implying that he has already beaten his man without a blow being struck. As the dance ends, the fighter walks back to his corner where his master is usually waiting on

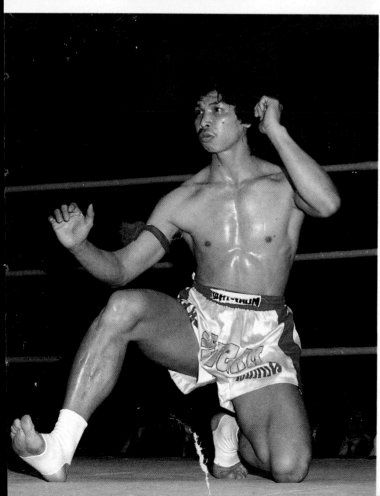

the other side of the ropes to whisper a special prayer of good luck to him. The prayer, strangely enough, is not uttered in the Thai language, but in Balinese. This blessing by his teacher is called 'the Buddha Breath'. When finished, the master blows three times on the fighter's forehead. In many Eastern cultures the forehead is said to be the seat of the third eye, the mystical eye of knowledge and understanding.

The Monkon

When a Thai boxing student has undergone his first twelve months of training he attends a special ceremony known as Teacher's Day. On this day all new students who have been training for a year have to formally approach the master of the camp bearing either a white flower or a small gift of silver. He officially asks the master if he will accept him as a student, and requests permission to represent the boxing school in the ring. The master, usually seated and dressed in white, decides whether or not the student can join the ranks. If the master does accept him, he will present the student with his own *monkon*. This is the traditional headband worn by all Thai boxers. Very great reverence is shown to it, and it also denotes that the student now has a teacher and belongs to a camp. After the ceremony the student swears an oath of allegiance to belong to that particular camp forever.

A ring name is then awarded to each accepted student. This is decided according to personal characteristics. The surname is the name of the camp he belongs to and that is why so many of the boxers seem to have the same surname.

The Thai Boxing Tournament

Specifications of the Thai boxing ring resemble those of international rings, together with a red corner and a blue corner. The weight categories are also similar to Western standards. Although officially fighters must be over 18 contestants as young as eight and nine years old fight for prize money in the rings. During all fights Thai music is played, with the tempo and volume varying to coincide with the action in the ring. Each bout consists of five 3-minute rounds, with two minutes break between each round. A boxer may win by a knockout, a technical knockout, or a decision. Thai boxing has a stringent code of ethics, and high mental and physical discipline is required of the contestants. Today muay thai is almost completely a contest art, as is sumo wrestling. The rigorous training, effective techniques, high conduct of sportsmanship, and unsurpassed courage have commanded the respect of other martial artists. Their unbeaten record is impressive, and to date there is no evidence of a well-ranked Thai boxer having been knocked out by a martial artist from any other style.

A Thai boxer using his technique to break wood by performing a jumping roundhouse kick about eight feet in the air.

Left *Thai boxing master Master Toddy demonstrating his incredible mental and physical powers. Standing with bare feet on broken glass aflame in gasoline, he is neither cut nor burned.*

Following pages *A twin-sword krabi-krabong fighter warms up before a fight.*

Krabi-Krabong, the Weapon Art of Thailand

Krabi-krabong is the revered art of Siamese sword and stick fighting. Its history is vague but it is believed to be more than 500 years old and stems from some form of army training. Fighting with the twin swords requires a great deal of skill. It takes a person nearly five years to learn all the basic techniques. A krabi-krabong match has no time limit and is truly a test of stamina and endurance. The bout ends only when the loser admits defeat and submits to his foe. Because the fighters wear no protective clothing or equipment, blood is often shed and injuries and torn garments are all quite normal. Cracked skulls, broken arms, legs and necks are also commonplace in these fights. As happened in kendo, the twin swords of krabi-krabong have today been replaced by hard wooden sticks. In a match, anything goes. If a weapon is lost or dropped the user can revert to judo-type throws or even kick and punch. The emphasis all the time is upon action.

Gambling and the Gangster Element in Muay Thai

Boxing in Thailand is big business with thousands of *baht* (dollars) changing hands at every tournament. Like most Asian peoples, the Thais are great gamblers. This leads to criminal involvement in the sport. Thai gangsters often threaten the lives of the participants and many fights are rigged. At a modern tournament in a big city it is not uncommon for a fighter's manager or his seconds to escort him into the ring armed with a pistol. A few years ago a famous Thai boxer who now lives in Europe had a brush with the Thai underworld.

Lose or Die

He was told that he had to stop winning fights because the racketeers were losing money heavily on his continued wins. One particular evening he was approached and informed that if he didn't throw that night's fight and take a dive in the third round he would not be alive the following morning. The Thai boxer was a simple country lad who had made good and was on his way to becoming national champion of his country. He was fiercely proud and refused to accede to the gangsters.

Out of the Shadows

So when he entered the ring for his fight, the young boxer went all out to win and in the second round he knocked his opponent out. He claimed the prize money and promptly left the ring. Later that night on his way home, two gangsters stepped out of the shadows and pumped three bullets into the brave boxer. Mercifully he survived the attack and within four months he was back in the ring. But he knew that his days must now be numbered so with discretion he left for Europe to teach the principles of muay thai there.

Right *At a martial arts of Thailand Festival two krabi -krabong fighters battle it out.*

Following pages, left *In krabi-krabong certain aspects of Thai boxing are involved and it is not unusual to see fighters employing kicks during a bout.*

Following pages, right *Krabi-krabong in traditional uniform battle with deadly efficiency. The blades are razor sharp and one false move could mean instant decapitation.*

The Burmese Art of Bando

Thailand's neighbor, Burma, has an art called *bando*, which closely resembles muay thai. It is not unreasonable to assume that because of the close historical association between these two countries, this sister art evolved from Thai boxing.

The general term for the Burmese martial arts is *thaing*, which means self-defense by both armed and unarmed methods. Bando is actually boxing by any other name.

Bando Techniques

Bando's techniques include the usual blocking and striking methods employed by many martial arts. But within the system there are also to be found grappling and locking techniques. After a student has learned the basic postures, which are based on 12 animals, similar to that of many kung fu styles, he than learns to develop his technique by sparring with other students. The roundhouse kick is delivered with the shin, just like in Thai boxing.

Bando in America

The bando system was introduced into America in the early 1960s by a Burmese doctor named Maung Gyi. Only one or two classes exist, the main one being at Georgia State University. Because the bando system is so versatile and has both a hard and soft subdivision, men and women can train in the various forms with little difficulty. Each of the animal styles in bando is specifically suited to people of certain strength, size, speed, and reactions. Once the instructor has determined a student's physical make up he can introduce him or her to the animal style that best suits them.

The Tiger of Bando

The tiger system of bando trains its adepts to behave like the animal itself. A fighting attitude is cultivated to characterize ferocious aggression, and this can be converted into a raging attack. The weapons of the tiger are its claws and jaws, so a student tries to emulate the animal by turning his fingers and thumb into claws for ripping and gouging the enemy. Attacks are usually directed towards the throat, neck, and face.

Way of the Disciplined

Bando means 'Way of the Disciplined'. Although practiced for hundreds of years in Burma it only came to prominence after a revival of national arts and warrior skills by the Japanese in 1941. There are 12 animals in the system, but the symbol of all the bando systems is the black panther. This animal was chosen for its fighting versatility.

Within the cobra techniques of bando lie all the lightning fast, paralysing nerve strikes. The cobra is considered to be the most difficult of all the bando animal systems to learn. Bando is a complete martial art, and is geared like most other Asian skills to develop the practitioner's inner qualities of tranquility and humility as well as building up his physique and fighting prowess.

Banshay

The Burmese forms of weapons arts are known as *banshay*. The main weapons are the short sword, staff, and spear. These all have sophisticated schools of technique. The Burmese swordsmen, unlike their Japanese counterparts, consider it bad form to kill or even injure an opponent. Their objective is merely to disarm an attacker without hurting him. Included within these weapon skills is also the bow-and-arrow.

The Weapons of the Martial Artist

The assimilation of learning is called knowledge, and the proper use of that knowledge is called wisdom.

Left *A three section staff showing that the user has to be versatile, and have knowledge of the hand arts before he is allowed to learn a weapon form.*

Right *The three sectional staff, a typical Chinese weapon, is very difficult to master. Novices experience constant injury during the early days of training.*

Every country in Asia over the centuries has developed its own forms of fighting arts. By far the greatest influence on them all has been China. Nevertheless many nations have their own indigenous fighting skills, developed through many hundreds of years by trial and error, adversity and the continued fight for freedom.

In the previous chapters we have learnt about many forms of empty hand styles and techniques. But not all martial arts are specifically empty hand ones. Some of them have become popular because of the weapon at the core of the system.

Pentjak-Silat

The national defense form of Indonesia is called *pentjak-silat*. It developed on the island of Sumatra sometime in the seventh century. Then over the years, by means of island-hopping from Sumatra to Java, and thence to Indonesia, the art influenced all who came into contact with it along the way. Ending up in Indonesia, it was further refined and developed. Today there are more than 150 distinct recorded styles of pentjak-silat. *Pentjak-silat* means 'to fight using skilled and specialized body movements'. The art encompasses armed and unarmed techniques. Because of its light and graceful movements it has often been classified as a dance but used against an enemy there is no doubt that it can be a deadly fighting art. When fighting, both arms are always in motion, as in a dance, but the eyes are focused on the opponent all the time. The extremely rapid movement of the pentjak-silat fighter tend to bemuse an opponent and the attack comes without warning. The fighter suddenly erupts into punches and kicks, striking at vital parts of the body before sweeping the opponent to the ground to finish him off.

The Legend of Silat

Legend ascribes the origin of pentjak-silat to a woman. Long ago in Sumatra a woman was sent down to the stream by her husband to fetch water. As she stooped to fill the bucket from the stream, she noticed a tiger attacking a huge bird. Fascinated, she watched the battle for several hours

until finally both animals died. Getting up to leave, she was suddenly confronted by her angry husband who had come down to the stream to see why his wife was taking so long fetching the water. The husband hit out at her in temper, but she evaded him easily, using the methods of the two animals she had just been watching. Her amazed husband stared back in disbelief as his every blow was either blocked or neutralized. Later on the wife taught her husband what she had learned, and pentjak-silat as an art was launched. To back up that old story, Sumatrans point out that there are still women today who are experts in the art.

The Muslim Tradition

Because pentjak-silat thrived in Islamic Sumatra, it has often been erroneously regarded as a strictly Muslim art, but this is not true, although most of its practitioners are Muslims. Because of its religious background, pentjak-silat has a profound philosophy behind it. All silat is influenced by the Koran, and the exponents of pentjak-silat strive through their martial art to seek *ihan*, or spiritual inspiration.

The Art as a Combat Form

Pentjak-silat used for combat training is referred to as *gayong* or *buah silat*. This kind of silat is a strange combination of delicate movement and forceful action. Combat silat dispenses with all that is not immediately related to practical result in hand-to-hand fighting. Every adept learns to protect himself from both armed and unarmed assailants, while he himself may be either armed or unarmed. As a result all training for combat silat involves the study of a wide range of weapons.

No Wages for the Teacher

Traditionally, the *guru* (teacher) of pentjak-silat accepted no payment from his pupils. He accepted just a token donation to keep him in clothes. The guru's skill existed only to be used to teach worthy disciples, and could not be used for profit. When a student wished to train in the art he was required to bring with him five offerings for the guru: a chicken, so that the blood from it could be spread on the training ground as a symbolic substitute for the student's own blood; a roll of white cloth for wrapping his body in, should the student die during training; a knife, to symbolize the student's sharpness; tobacco, so that the teacher could smoke during his rest period; and finally, a little money to replace the teacher's clothes, should they be ripped in practice.

Once accepted, the disciple swore an oath on the Koran, and became a blood brother to all the other students.

The Harimau Style

The most popular style of silat in Sumatra is called *harimau*, and resembles the antics of a tiger. Because of the damp conditions in the area where this particular style originated

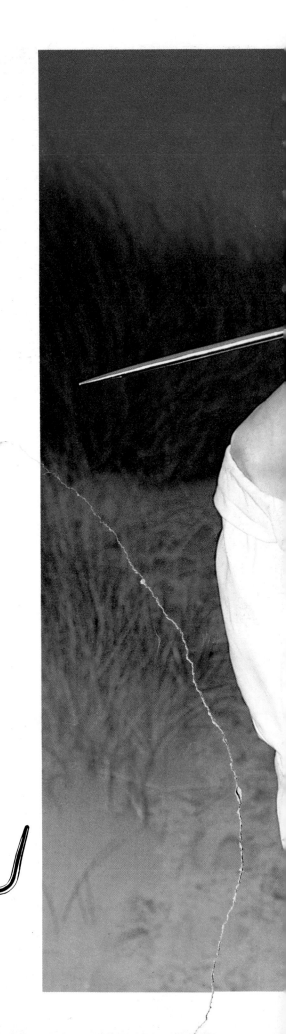

Left *A karateka holds aloft twin sai. This Okinawan weapon is much used today in the performance of kata. It is an effective weapon when used against a bo staff or even a samurai sword.*

Following page *The twin sticks of escrima or arnis de mano. One of America's top instructors Danny Inosanto (right) demonstrates the trapping capability of the art.*

a normal upright stance and movement were discarded in favor of ground-hugging movements. A combatant crouches close to the ground and inches his body forwards until he is within striking range. This style requires great strength and flexibility in the hips and legs.

Malaysian Bersilat

Malaysian bersilat is derived from Indonesian pentjak-silat which it resembles. But in spite of this, it is technically different in many ways. The name *bersilat* means 'to do, by fighting'. The art is divided into two styles. One is a dance form that is displayed on public holidays. This has lost much of its fighting realism and is practiced merely for the grace and poise it develops. The other style is known as *buah* and this is a hard, effective combat method that is never publicly seen. Buah, the combat side of bersilat, contains techniques which make considerable use of the legs and looks quite acrobatic in nature. The secrecy that surrounds this art ensures that only the most dedicated and select students know its innermost mysteries. The vows they take forbid them to divulge anything that they learn.

Modern bersilat

In Malaya, bersilat training is considered to be a perfect physical exercise and a sport. It is taught in schools and colleges throughout the peninsula. This modern version of the art has nothing like the combative value its ancestor had, and is really quite diluted. It is only in remote areas and the outer islands that the true bersilat still exists, and that is not open to the eyes of anyone except the true devotee.

Filipino Kali

Records dating back to AD 750 indicate that the ancient peoples of the Philippines had developed a highly specialized form of weapon fighting. *Kali* comes from a Malay word meaning 'bladed weapon'. In learning this art, one starts by learning about the weapon first and the empty-hand method last. The weapon concerned is the machete-like knife known as the *bolo*. With this in one hand and a dagger in the other, the kali practitioner was an awesome sight in battle, as Ferdinand Magellan found out when he invaded the island of Cebu in 1521. Even though the attacking Spaniards had far superior weapons, they were defeated by natives bearing knives and sticks.

Arnis de Mano

Although kali was the ancient martial art of the Philippines, it is the Spanish term *arnis de mano*, 'harness of the hand', that describes the self-defense system of the Philippines. This art in the main uses twin sticks and bladed weapons. Arnis also goes under another name, *escrima* which means 'skirmish' in Spanish. By whatever name it goes under, it is one of the deadliest fighting arts of the Orient.

Spanish Conquest

When the Spaniards invaded the Philippines, they had a hard time imposing their rule on the inhabitants and were constantly attacked by razor-sharp bolos, twin sticks, and daggers. It was only through the use of firearms that the invaders could bring about any semblance of order. When finally Spanish rule was firmly established the conquerors set about banning the learning and teaching of arnis de mano. The carrying of the bolo was also forbidden in an attempt to minimize the heavy death toll among the occupying troops. The art of escrima or arnis de mano went underground, as did karate in Okinawa when the occupying Japanese issued similar edicts. The art eventually re-emerged and went unnoticed by the Spaniards because it had been set to music and resembled a dance.

Constant Rebellion

Because the art was learned in secret (some classes were even taught by moonlight) and because many of the hundreds of islands were widely separated and hosted different languages, many styles grew up independently of each other. Much to their dismay, the Spanish invaders found themselves under constant harassment from the Morro tribesmen's guerrilla tactics. These tactics persisted on and off for nearly 300 years of Spanish colonization.

The USA Steps in

When the United States won the Spanish-American War the Filipinos thought they would get self-rule. But the islands were too strategically valuable, so Americans merely replaced the Spaniards. Although the Philippines now had a new benevolent master, the fierce Morro natives would not be subjugated. Their ferocious fighting techniques, using twin sticks and bolo knives, exacted a deadly toll of the lives of the American marines occupying the islands.

Black Jack Pershing

To try and put an end to the losses suffered by his troops, General Pershing issued a special leather neck-covering for his men. This protected them from having their throats cut and helped to lower the terrifying casualty rate. This is why the US marines are known the world over as 'leathernecks'.

Migration to America

During World War Two it was the Japanese who felt the sting of the Filipino martial arts. The tribesmen alongside American service personnel fought with their ancient blades and twin sticks to defeat the Japanese occupying forces. After the war, many Filipinos emigrated to the United States. Needless to say, their arnis de mano went with them. Most of the immigrants went to Hawaii and California. Of those that went to California, the majority settled in Stockton and it was there that arnis de mano/escrima surfaced onto the American martial arts scene.

Influence of Bruce Lee

The discovery of escrima must be credited to the late Bruce Lee because his portrayal of the use of double sticks in the movie *Enter the Dragon* and the unfinished *Game of Death* brought the art of Filipino stick-fighting out into the open. Bruce Lee was taught the art of escrima by his long-time friend and student Danny Inosanto. Danny in turn had been trained by a distinguished escrimador in Stockton.

Escrima Tactics

A tactic in escrima called *retirada*, or "retreating' style, is designed for encounters where the fighter has time and room to keep backing away in order to study his opponent's movements. When a fighter is forced to make a stand, the opposite tactic is used — the *fondo fuerte,* or 'non-retreating' style. All the footwork in escrima works on the lines of a triangle. The triangular footwork comes into its own when a person is attacked with his back to the wall with no prospects of moving anywhere. This doesn't make the slightest difference to an escrimador because a triangle fits into a corner perfectly. In other words, he is never trapped because he is used to working on the triangular pattern.

The Song of the Butterfly

Most students of escrima and kali somewhere along the way in their training learn the use of a little knife known as the *balisong*, or 'butterfly knife'. This Filipino knife dates back more than 1000 years. Legend has it that a great Filipino warrior trained in the martial art of kali and armed solely with this small razor-sharp folding knife, took on in mortal combat 29 enemy warriors — and killed them all. The native word for the blade is *veintinueve*, which means 'twenty-nine' and it commemorates that great feat. The knife actually took its name from a *barrio* in the Philippines called Balisung. *Bali* means 'to break', and *sung* means 'horn'. The people of that town are said to have been the first to produce the broken horn knife.

This was first introduced into the States by the early immigrant farm workers, and later by returning GIs who brought them home as war souvenirs. Because of the click-click noise made by the knife when it is flicked open, second-generation Filipino American children likened the sound to that of a butterfly rubbing its wings. As a result, it became known as the butterfly knife. Another version of the name's origin and perhaps a little more believable than listening to the sound of a butterfly rubbing its wings together, is that when the knife is half-open it resembles a butterfly in flight.

The Bali-Song Today

During the 1950s and 1960s the knife gained a bad image because it resembled a switchblade. But during the kung fu boom of the early 1970s, the Bali-Song once again became respectable. The butterfly knife has twin handles that when folded completely envelop the blade, thus eliminating the

Sensei Inoue demonstrating Bo Kata.

need for a sheath. The knife is opened by a flick of the wrist and the handles revolve in opposite directions to be caught in the user's hand and held together for a solid grip. The martial arts world took to this weapon immediately. Hollywood too, saw its potential and used experts such as Danny Inosanto and Jeff Imada to create film sequence fight scenes. The 1981 Burt Reynolds movie *Sharkey's Machine* contained such a sequence using the butterfly knife. Today the knife has been patented by Les de Asis and the name Bali-Song has been officially registered.

The Art of India

In southern India in the province of Kerala, there is practiced an art called Kalaripayit. *Kalaripayit* means 'battlefield training'. A *Kalari* is the place where the participants practice and is the equivalent of a Karate dojo. There are two distinct styles: the northern style, which is very hard and is practiced by the Nayers who are the warrior caste; and the southern style, which is dominated by the Tamils. Because the country is so vast, the two styles are quite noticeably different.

Northern and Southern Styles

In the north the Kalaripayit is tremendously energetic. Participants kick about eight feet into the air with their legs vertical. They do exercises in which one minute the leg is absolutely vertical, right up in the air, and the next minute come crashing down into a complete splits. The Kalari measures exactly 21 ft by 42 ft. There is endless salutation and bowing to gods and altars. In the south, the style is rugged and the stances are much shorter. It has a crude look to it, being less supple and energetic.

The Foundations

The martial art of Kalaripayit is based on a series of ancient documents called *Sastras*. These are secret writings passed on through the ages and written on palm scrolls. They list 108 vital points on the body which if struck, will cause death. The system is very similar to Japanese Atemi. This dark side of the art is termed *Marma-adi* and it is taught only to the most advanced students. A peculiar aspect of the northern style is that all practice is conducted at night and in secret.

The Evil Eye

Because of its advanced techniques Marma-adi has become a separate branch of the art of Kalaripayit. A master of Marma-adi does not teach exercises or forms, he concentrates only on teaching the vital points and resuscitation techniques. A certain amount of fear has grown among villages through the ages about the metaphysical powers of these masters. A sort of witchdoctor image has been conjured up, and it is said that if someone offends a Marma-adi master, he only has to look that person straight in the eye in order to kill him. It perhaps lends truth to the old saying, 'if looks could kill'. All masters of Kalaripayit are traditional doctors in their own right.

The Village Art

Kalaripayit is still mostly a village art, but on a huge scale. There are at least 500 schools practicing in southern India alone. The art was practiced in secret under the British, during their colonization of India in the last century and, as far as is known, Kalaripayit is purely indigenous to India. Students of the art are not allowed to train in it before they have undergone a month of special massage to get their bodies into a receptive state. The only type of uniform worn is a pelvic girdle that acts like a truss and supports the groin. This bandage-like contraption measures 40 feet in length, and is applied to the body by first tying the end round a tree trunk. Then the students wind themselves up in it like a cocoon.

Training in Kalaripayit

The art on the whole is very tough. Throws are practiced on solid stone floors. It also includes a very fast form of shadow boxing. On the soft side, it involves lots of throws and locks. Kalaripayit also has a complex weapons system that includes hundreds of disarming techniques, as well as all combinations of unarmed combat. In both styles there are four main categories, beginning with unarmed techniques, then training with bamboo twin sticks, followed by knives, spears, and swords. It ends with learning the vital secrets of the mystical Marma-adi. Kalaripayit is riddled with religious overtones — so much so that on occasions when there have been no students the Kalari has been turned into a temple, or a sacred lamp is lit every day and it is just left. A Kalari is never pulled down.

Students of the art must be obedient, they must respect Kali the goddess of war, and always show proper respect to their master.

The Cult of Thuggee

During the latter part of the nineteenth century in India, there arose a group or cult of fanatics who practiced the killer art of *thuggee*. These people were rebelling against the British. At one time they had all been practitioners of Kalaripayit, and were masters of Marma-adi. To create havoc and fear amongst the British, they would steal into the British camps and barracks at dead of night and strangle soldiers by means of a silken scarf with a rupee coin encased within its folds. Death came quickly and silently, as the solid coin pressed against the victim's throat. These Indian fanatics claimed their goddess Kali had ordered them to do this in order to clear the British from India. The word 'thug' is derived from these ancient killers of Bombay, where the strongest thuggee sects existed. To Western eyes these methods may seem a little drastic — a misuse of the martial arts, perhaps. But to the followers of the cult, they were only doing what seemed natural to them — to rid their land of the forces of occupation by every possible means.

Weapons of the Artists

Weapons are as much part of the martial arts as the empty hand techniques related to those systems. The traditional weapons techniques as practiced today are deemed of great value to the martial arts practitioner. These ancient tools of warfare serve the modern martial artist in his quest to gain mastery over himself and his art.

Every oriental fighting method has within its system some form of weapon or weapons section. Some of these latter-day instruments of war, to Western eyes, look rather curious. But in the hands of an expert, simple farming implements become lethal weapons.

The Sai — Horn of Death

The sai is today a weapon very much promoted by the karate movement. Traditionally Okinawa was the home of this weapon but it is also found throughout Southeast Asia, from India to the Philippines. It is a short-range weapon much resembling a trident, usually made of iron, and measuring 15 to 20 inches long.

Although looking like a very short sword, the tip is actually blunt. About one-third of the way down the shaft, two opposing prongs or tines are used as a handle to grip the weapon with. The sai, usually used in pairs, was capable of killing or maiming an enemy with a blow to the back of the neck, or a thrust to the throat or at the eyes. The butt or pommel of the sai was often used for stiking at nerve points or at the temple. There are only two basic ways of gripping the sai — one is to hold it with the blade pointing outward, and the other is with the blade pointing inward.

The nunchaku or rice flails are the best known of all the martial arts weapons. Made popular in recent years by the late Bruce Lee, this weapon when used correctly can keep several attackers at bay. In the wrong hands the nunchaku can kill and it is banned in many places.

The Sai in Japan

The sai requires rigid training and great skill to manipulate it. When it was first introduced to Japan, it was adopted by the police force and used as a sort of iron truncheon. The Japanese police found it very effective in blocking the thrusts of the Samurai's razor-sharp blades. During arrests it was used against criminals' pressure points in order to subdue them. Later, the Japanese altered the shape of the sai by losing one of the prongs. They then renamed it the jutte. This weapon was used by the police for a considerable time, until it was dropped in favor of the gun.

The Sai in Karate

It is said that the Brahmic god Indra, who was the guardian of holy places, especially temples, carried a crude version of what appeared to be a sai. Its use spread across Asia in one form or another. In Indonesia it is known as the tjabang, in China they call it the titkio. But this ancient weapon has finally found its acknowledged home in karate. One of the leading practitioners of the sai in the United States is the Japanese master, Fumio Demura.

Today, when the sai are used by karateka, they are made from tempered steel instead of iron. Although no longer used as a weapon in the strictest terms, a karateka wielding them in performance of the special sai kata known as *jigen* during a tournament demonstration makes a dazzling sight. His wrists and hands flick through the difficult movements with amazing dexterity.

A recent version of this weapon is the telescopic sai. This is a series of tubes within tubes, all metal. When flicked downwards by the wrist, it is transformed into a foot-long steel truncheon. This weapon is becoming increasingly popular as a form of protection against muggers.

The Nunchaku

The nunchaku was originally used as an agricultural tool to flail rice, but it was later developed on the island of Okinawa as a weapon during the Japanese occupation. Here again is a weapon that was thought to be purely indigenous to Okinawa, but in fact the nunchaku is to be seen all over Asia. It consists of two equal lengths of hardwood held together at the top by a cord or chain. The pieces of wood are about 12 to 15 inches long. The simple look of the apparatus disguises a truly awesome weapon. The nunchaku can be used to block or parry, or it can be swung with terrible force to deliver smashing blows at an assailant from long range. The cord that holds it together is used for choking.

The Springing Tiger

In present day martial arts no weapon has earned for itself more notoriety than the nunchaku. The *chuks* as they are sometimes called, are considered by the police and courts to be offensive weapons. At first glance two pieces of wood strung together by a length of cord may not look too

Below *A traditional Okinawan yari or spear. Weapons such as this can be found in virtually every civilization on earth. Only the Japanese have turned the use of this weapon into a fine art.*

fearsome a weapon. But in the hands of a skilled practitioner the nunchaku can be likened to an unleashed tiger springing into action and leaving carnage in its wake. It has been said that a pair of nunchaku used by an expert can keep several men at bay simultaneously.

20th Century Street Weapon

When the nunchaku is in motion it is nearly impossible to grab it and take it away from the person wielding it. Blocks can be delivered in two places at the same time. It is a weapon that can be used at a distance and also at close quarters. This simple farming implement, once used for threshing grain by the people of Okinawa, has been developed and refined to become an awesome street weapon of the twentieth century. But there are two facets to this ancient weapon. Apart from being an instant injury implement, the nunchaku in the hands of a serious and dedicated karateka can be a source of inspiration for kata, and a dynamic tool for improving the martial artist's training regimen. Interestingly enough, when the nunchaku are used by an untrained person, they usually cause more harm to the wielder than to the attacker.

The early nunchaku's were held together by rope plaited and braided from horse tails. It was a weapon that was easy to conceal and yet with a flick of the wrist it could be drawn out and used with deadly efficiency. Its construction was simple. It is fairly safe to assume that the early development of the nunchaku both as an agricultural implement and a weapon originated in China. Variants of it are seen in the Philippines, where it is known by the name of *tabak-toyok*, in Vietnam, Laos, Cambodia, and Malaysia.

Adoption by Karate

Like the sai, the nunchaku was adopted primarily by students of karate. The karate man who had already developed agility, found the use of nunchaku in training extremely effective. The fast moves and quick thinking required with the use of this weapon add a bonus to martial arts training in general. Although the chuks were known and used by karateka in the United States for a number of years, it was Hollywood and Bruce Lee's first American film, *Enter the Dragon*, that brought the weapon its universal popularity and notoriety. Bruce Lee's skill with the nunchaku in the movie encouraged kids all over the country to construct a pair of their own, just like that of their hero.

The Law Steps In

Within weeks, the nunchaku craze had swept across America. There were unfortunate accidents resulting from unskilled attempts to use something that requires a great deal of skill. But criminals also saw the potential of nunchaku, and jumped on the bandwagon. Before long, assaults, muggings, and similar villainnies were being executed by the use of the easily constructed nunchaku.

Then the law stepped in and made it an offense to carry the nunchaku because it was classified as a deadly weapon. Within months it had been outlawed. States such as California simply amended their existing laws to include the nunchaku. On 4 April 1974 Article 2 of the California penal code made it an imprisonable offense even to carry nunchaku, without actually using them.

Exceptions to the Rule

For a while it looked as though, thanks to misuse, the dedicated karateka would have to forego his or her valuable nunchaku training. But in the subdivision of the penal code the law stated that there would be certain exceptions. It went on to state that nunchaku could be used on proper licensed premises in the confines of a martial arts school or club when used in the practice of a system of self-defense or karate. So it seems that, for martial artists at least, the nunchaku has been saved.

The Tonfa

The tonfa, sometimes called the *tui-fa*, was originally the handle used to turn a manually operated millstone. It had a shaft about 20 inches in length, with a grip attached to it about one-fourth of the way down. It was used as a weapon by gripping the handle, so that the shorter end extended past the knuckles. The longer end swung out freely from under the arm to hit its target. As with the sai, the tonfa can be used either singly or in pairs. It is made of white oak and weighs about $1\frac{1}{4}$ pounds. In martial arts circles it is only karate people who use this weapon. In the old days in Okinawa, students had to be Third Dan black belts or better, before they were allowed to train with it.

Modern Use of the Tonfa

During the late 1960s, when American karateka began to adopt the tonfa as part of their training curriculum, law enforcement agencies and the marines began to take notice of this simple Oriental weapon. A deputy sheriff by the name of Lon Anderson recalled an incident he had seen when serving in Okinawa. He had witnessed a native policeman, virtually single-handed, put down a minor village riot. The policeman had gone into the thick of the mob whirling a pair of tonfa sticks. Striking out left and right at legs and arms, he quickly quelled the riot. Anderson thought that if that could be done in the Orient, the same could be done in America.

The Prosecutor — PR 21 Baton

With thought and ingenuity Lon Anderson redesigned the ancient mill handle. The original had been short and slightly oval. Anderson made it longer, to become about the same length as the regular police baton. He extended the handle, and instead of using wood, as in the original tonfa, he used black fiberglass and made it completely round in shape. He named it the PR 21 prosecutor stick. Right from

its introduction, police forces were quick to recognize the extra protection afforded to them by the prosecutor stick. By 1972 major police agencies from Los Angeles to Rochester, New York, adopted the PR 21 baton as standard issue, to replace their time-honored billy clubs. In a typical knife assault officers have found that the prosecutor stick is more than adequate. In the past, an officer in a similar situation may have had to resort to his pistol.

Since this weapon has replaced the law officers' billy club or night stick, the military police have also adopted it.

The Peacemaker

The psychological impact of the prosecutor stick is nearly as powerful as the physical punishment it can mete out. This works in two ways — it deters physical confrontation by giving the user the confidence to come across with more authority; and it also keeps the peace without an officer having to resort to violence. It is also a very useful crowd disperser, used either as a short or medium range weapon. So far as is known, the United States is the only Western country to have made use of this karate weapon as an aid to its law enforcement agencies.

The Kubotan

A scaled-down version of the tonfa available for civilian use is a little weapon known as the *kubotan*. The kubotan was invented by a Japanese sensei and weapons expert named Takayuki Kubota. It is a 5½-inch cylindrical piece of solid plastic that is often disguised as a key ring. When applied in arm and joint locks, or at nerve points it produces immediate excruciating pain. Sensei Kubota developed a special series of self-defense techniques to accompany the use of this weapon in his capacity as an unarmed combat instructor and advisor to the Federal Bureau of Investigation. Sensei Kubota introduced the little weapon into the training program with the most amazing results. Master Kubota is also under permanent contract as a police defense training instructor at the LAPD Academy.

The Kama

The *kama* is a short sickle with a hardwood handle. At first glance it looks much like the kind of sickle that has been used for centuries in both Eastern and Western farming cultures. The tool is used for harvesting rice or cutting hay. But to the farmers of Okinawa it proved to be a valuable

Left *The tonfa — originally a handle from a rice grinder — has found new usage. In many places an adaptation of the tonfa has replaced the policeman's old-time night stick or billy club.*

Right *The steel-bladed kama or rice sickle can be used singly or in pairs. For demonstration purposes the blades are made of oak.*

Below *The Kubotan keyring is an ingenious device that can be used to hit an attacker's nerve points or even in a strangulation hold.*

defense aid when the Japanese banned all weapons.

Farmers took their kamas, sharpened them to a razor's edge, then developed a series of defense measures by using the kama in pairs. Many a Samurai has fallen foul of twin kamas when picking on a seemingly defenseless peasant. Today, as with a lot of these ancient weapons, they have found new life in the modern martial arts, only now they are made entirely of wood, even the blade.

Kusarigama — Swirling Chain of Death

Man's ingenuity for defending himself knows no bounds, adaptability being the byword. The *kamma* or common sickle was upgraded by the Japanese peasant to become a formidable weapon known as the *kusarigama*. This was a tool that could be used to challenge a sword-wielding Samurai on his own terms. Basically, the kusarigama was a sickle with a length of chain between 4 and 15 feet long, with one end attached to the handle and the other fixed to a heavy steel ball. The ball measured about 2 inches in diameter. The idea was to whirl the ball and chain around a swordsman's arms and thus to ensnare him. This made it possible for the peasant to move in close and decapitate him with the kama. The action was similar to that of the *bolas*, used by the South American gaucho.

Right *Wooden kama are an essential part of the modern karatika's arsenal when performing kata with weapons.*

Left *The ancient Chinese chain whip was originally a battlefield weapon. Wielding it, a mounted soldier could keep several infantrymen at bay.*

Left *The kwan do or Knife of General Kwan. Today the kwan do has be relegated to a display weapon.*

Right *The samurai sword in the thrust position.*

Sealed in Blood

The weapon came into being around the mid-1500s in Japan. It was adopted by the martial arts fraternities of the day, but was quickly dropped because of the extreme difficulty of its use. One school, however, retained it and expanded its techniques in use to such an extent that within 50 years a kusarigama could be used effectively against a Samurai armed with twin swords. Students flocked to the school to learn the use of this wierd and wonderful weapon, but acceptance was very strict because a novice student had to sacrifice many things in order to join. He had to pledge secrecy. He was not allowed to drink alcohol, nor when proficient at a later date was he allowed to open his own school. He must never argue with other school members, nor think or speak badly of his master. If knowledge of kusarigama techniques ever leaked out, it could be a matter of life and death, because an enemy could then develop counter-techniques. When a student had sworn to uphold this strict code of secrecy he was expected to seal a document with his own blood. This was performed by pricking the second knuckle on the student's left hand. If after this a student ever disclosed any of the school's secrets, he would be put to death in a very painful way.

Kwan Do, the Knife of General Kwan

In the Chinese weapons systems, the traditional kwan do is surely the most impressive. The weapon is a curved blade between 18 and 24 inches long. It is mounted on the top of a 5-foot staff, with a metal point fitted to the bottom end. Legend states that it was invented by a Chinese general named Kwan Yu. General Kwan is often regarded as the patron saint of the Chinese martial arts because of his virtuous life and military skill. The original kwan do was said to weigh in the region of 120 pounds, and from all accounts was a mighty weapon. The kwan do is a long-range weapon.

Bring Me the Head of Hua Hsiung

General Kwan spent his life performing great deeds. On one occasion he presented himself in front of a powerful king whom was having trouble with a mighty warrior called Hua Hsiung. Hua Hsiung had already killed two of the greatest fighters in the kingdom. General Kwan offered his services to the king, stating that if he failed to kill the rebel Hua Hsiung, he would offer his own head in exchange. Then grabbing his powerful weapon he rode off to engage the rebel chief in battle. A short time later General

Kwan returned and threw the rebel leader's head at the feet of the king.

Today the kwan do can be seen in most kung fu schools, where its use in training develops the martial spirit.

The Sword of the Samurai

The sword or *katana* was the basic weapon of the Samurai class. Before AD 700, the blades were straight, but after that time they became curved in design and have remained so ever since. Making the sword was an art in itself, and once finished, the product was of the highest quality. The sword, like the cowboy's six-shooter, was with the owner at all times. There is no other country in the world where the sword has received so much honor and renown as in Japan. It became known as the very soul of the warrior class. All Samurais carried two swords, one long, one short.

Testing the Cut

When not fighting, warriors would test their swords and cutting skills by a method known as *tameshigiri,* which required the use of corpses of decapitated criminals. The corpses were used either singly or in groups. By these methods the Samurai developed many diversified cutting styles. They would continually chop at the corpses until they had been reduced to pieces the size of a man's hand. Most Samurai would practice up to 3000 cuts a day, just to keep themselves up to scratch. If another warrior happened to brush past a Samurai and accidentally touched his sword, he would be instantly challenged. If the offender were a common peasant, he would have been instantly struck down and killed. This was permissible right up until 1876. Then an edict was passed forbidding the Samurai to wear his traditional twin swords.

The Iron Fan

A very popular weapon in the Chinese schools of martial arts was the iron fan. As a weapon, the fan was short and very convenient. It was carried daily for cooling purposes, but besides fanning the breeze, it could be used to kill an enemy. As a result, it's possessor was perpetually armed. The fan was constructed very like the standard paper one except that the paper was glued to iron strips instead of bamboo. It was used for stabbing, lifting, and plucking. The striking power was generated from the wrists. Experts in its use could, if the occasion required, splay the fan out, and hurl it at an enemy to knock his head right off.

Left *The lance, known in Japan as the yari, was the basic armament of the southeast Asian foot soldier in ancient times.*

Right, above *The attacker moves to strike with the yari or spear.*

Right, below *The sword wielder deflects this long-range weapon with blade of his katana or sword.*

Left and below *Two karateka fighting with a bo staff and sword. Although the sword looks the deadlier weapon, a bo staff in the hands of an expert can be more lethal.*

Right *The Chinese saber was standard issue a thousand years ago in the court of the emperor. Nowadays it can be seen to dominate many of the wu shu demonstrations seen around the world.*

Left *The tiger fork, also known as the trident, is an ancient Chinese weapon that today is relegated to demonstration only. Yet not too many years ago these forks were actually used to hunt tigers.*

Right *The wu shu jien is the classic sword of the Chinese emperor's guard. Today it is used in tai-chi demonstrations.*

Chinese Swords and Other Weapons

The *wu shu jien* or *gim* is China's double-edged sword with a straight blade. Today this weapon is in constant use with the practitioners of tai chi chuan. They use it as an extension of their art. It is a beautiful weapon that has a long colored tassle hanging from its hilt. This was always removed before any actual fighting began.

The tiger fork, or trident, is a long spearlike weapon used originally to kill tigers with in southern China. It eventually became a martial arts weapon and can often be seen accompanying lion dance groups when they perform their celebration ritual.

The short, wide-bladed butterfly knives are seen in many kung fu styles. These should not be confused with the Filipino balisong, which is quite different. The *darn do* or butterfly knives are one of the only two weapons used in the kung fu system of wing chun although choy-li-fut has a similar weapon. Its popularity was probably due to the fact that crowded urban conditions made such a compact weapon desirable.

the *bo* staff, also known as a cudgel in China, really needs no introduction at all. This weapon can be seen in cultures the world over, although Asiatic peoples put much more emphasis on its use than Westerners ever did.

Conclusion

Many other weapons and unarmed arts that we have not mentioned exist in the world today. These include the foot fighters of Brazil with their art of capoeira born out of slavery.

The sambo wrestlers of the Balkans, the Greco-Roman wrestlers, and the quarterstaff fighters of medieval Britain. The list is almost endless, country by country.

Of one thing we can be certain, warfare and fighting in general have progressed at terrifying speed. In contrast with the early days of the martial arts, when they were first developing, modern technology has changed weaponry out of all recognition. But thanks to a dedicated band of martial arts practitioners in the Orient, a valuable legacy of fighting styles has been handed down and preserved for us to practice and appreciate in the twentieth century.

"Life unfolds on a great sheet called time, and once finished is gone forever."...Old Chinese Proverb

Shidoshi Stephen Hayes, universally recognized as the father of American ninjutsu, poses with the ninja sword.

Right   The mystical kujikuri ninja hand sign. Each hand sign is said to invoke the power of that sign to the user, the signs including water, fire and earth.

GLOSSARY

Acupuncture Ancient Chinese system of healing using needles at certain key points of the body to effect a cure.

Aikido Japanese martial art of which there are many styles. The most popular is Ueshiba, named after its founder, Morehei Ueshiba.

Arnis de mano Filipino martial art involving twin short hard wooden sticks.

Atemi Japanese art of attacking and striking the vital points of the body.

Balisong Butterfly knife, small switchblade-type knife opened by a downward wrist action. Used in the Philippines with deadly efficiency.

Bando Burmese boxing method.

Bersilat Malayan martial art also practiced in Indonesia and Sumatra. Present day emphasis is more on the sporting form.

Black Belt The black belt indicates that the student has reached a level of proficiency in certain martial arts, in order to teach himself.

Bodhidharma Indian monk also known as *Ta'mo*, the legendary instigator of kung fu at the original Shaolin temple.

Bok Hok Pai White crane style of kung fu.

Bokken Solid wooden sword used for training purposes.

Bok Mei Pai White eyebrow style of kung fu.

Buddhism Eastern religion which spread from India to China, then to many parts of Asia. Various branches or sects exist as offshoots.

Bushi Japanese term meaning 'warrior'

Bushido 'Way of the warrior'. It was also a very strict Samurai code of ethics based on honor, loyalty, duty, and obedience.

Butterfly Knives Also known as *bot jum do*. Short knives used in pairs in kung fu systems.

Center Line Imaginary line running down the center of the body, the location of many vital points.

Chan or Ch'an Chinese word for Zen. the word means 'meditation'. In India it is known as *Dhyana*.

Chan San Feng Legendary founder of tai chi chuan, one of the internal schools of Chinese boxing.

Chi or Chi-Gung Internal energy; a special set of exercises to develop inner strength.

Chi Sao Exercise in wing chun kung fu for building co-ordination and sensitivity; also teaches correct elbow positioning.

Choy Li Fut Southern Chinese form of Shaolin kung fu.

Chuan Chinese term meaning 'fist'.

Chudan In Japanese martial arts, the middle area or chest.

Crane One of the five animal styles in Shaolin kung fu.

Dan Japanese term for anyone who has achieved the rank of black belt or higher.

Daruma Japanese name for the Indian monk Bodhidharma. Known as *Ta'mo* in China.

Dim Mak The death touch. A delayed action strike that can kill a victim hours or days after the blow has been struck.

Do In Japanese means 'way' or 'path', identified with Chinese tao.

Dojo Training hall or place used for practicing Japanese martial arts.

Dragon One of five animal styles of Shaolin kung fu. The dragon symbolizes spirit.

Drunken Monkey System of kung fu in which a practitioner staggers to fool an opponent into thinking he is intoxicated.

Elbow Close quarter technique, used in martial arts. Also much favored by Thai boxers who know it as sok.

Empty Hand Literal meaning of karate in Japanese.

Escrima A Filipino martial art using sticks, swords, and daggers. the word is Spanish and means 'skirmish'. Also known as Arnis de mano.

Five Ancestors The five survivors of the original Shaolin temple after it was sacked.

Form Series of choreographed movements incorporating many martial arts techniques. It is a set of patterns aimed at improving the practitioner's application of technique.

Free Fighting Exercise in all martial arts similar to sparring. A fighter uses his own interpretation of techniques to beat his opponent.

Full Contact A form of karate where full power kicks are delivered at an opponent. Contestants wear boxing gloves, and pads on their feet.

Gedan Lower area of the body, in Japanese martial arts.

Genin Lowest rank of the three classifications of the ninja. Genin were the ones who performed the assassinations.

Gi Training uniform used by practitioners of the Japanese martial arts. In karate it is known as a karate-gi, in judo a judo-gi.

Gichin Funakoshi founder of shotokan karate. He was instrumental in introducing karate into Japan from Okinawa.

Gojo-Ryu One of the major styles of karate developed from Okinawan naha-te. It is a hard and soft system.

Gung Fu Common name for the Chinese martial arts, also pronounced kung fu.

Guru In pentjak-silat, the traditional teacher of the art. Of Muslim or Indian origin.

Hakama Long divided skirt covering the legs and feet. Used in aikido and many other Japanese martial arts.

Hapkido Korean martial art involving kicks and hand strikes, meaning 'the way of harmony'.

Hari-Kiri Japanese ritual suicide by disembowelment. Proper term is seppuku.

Honbu Headquarters of the different Japanese martial arts.

Hsing-I Chinese soft or internal kung fu art.

Hung Gar One of the five ancestor styles of kung fu.

Hwarang Do 'The way of the flowering manhood'. A code similar to bushido used in Korea by members of the Hwarang. Hwarang-do is now a much practiced martial art.

Hyung One of the basics of taekwondo training; the practice of forms or patterns.

Iai-Do Japanese martial art of drawing and re-sheathing the *katana* or sword. It is a noncombat art descended from iai-jutsu. It stresses intellectual and spiritual attainment.

I-Ching The Chinese *Book of Changes*. This ancient book is consulted even today for telling the future. The teachings of the I-Ching form the philosophical basis of tai chi chuan.

Iga An area in Japan known for its remoteness in medieval times. Home of one of the many schools of ninja.

Iron Palm Lethal technique known in kung fu for its ability to kill with a single blow. Much conditioning is required over several years to make the adept's hand and arm like iron. Not to be confused with dim mak.

Jiu Jitsu Ancient Japanese form of warrior training, including both armed and unarmed techniques. The term means 'soft' or 'flexible'.

Jodan In Japanese martial arts, the top area of the body, i.e. from the shoulders upwards.

Jonin Highest rank in the ninja echelon.

Judo Modern sport form of jiu jitsu. Developed by Dr Jigoro Kano in 1882. The sport form uses the opponent's own strength to his disadvantage.

Judoka One who practices judo.

Jutsu Japanese word meaning 'skill' or 'art'.

Kalaripayit Indian method of combat. The term means 'battle place' or 'field'.

Kama The sickle, a weapon developed in Okinawa.

Karate Japanese martial art developed from Chinese systems. It is a means of self-defense for an unarmed person using strikes and kicks aimed at the body.

Karateka One who trains in karate.

Kata In karate, a pre-set series of movements in which the practitioner defends himself against imaginary opponents.

Kempo Japanese pronunciation of *chuan'fa*, which is Chinese for 'way of the fist'. Kempo is a type of Chinese and Korean karate based on high speed blocks and counterattacks.

Kendo Modern Japanese fencing based on the warrior skill of kenjutsu. In kendo practitioners fight with bamboo shinai.

Ki Japanese word for the internal intrinsic energy within the body. Ki is the Japanese translation of the Chinese chi. Ki is the inner power.

Krabi-Krabong Armed combat system of Thailand. Adepts fight with twin swords or sword and shield.

Kung Fu All the fighting arts of China. It is a slang generic term meaning 'a person of attainment', or 'one who works or exercises to the highest of his ability'. It was adopted erroneously by Westerners then became accepted and used by the Chinese themselves.

Kup In taekwon-do, the eight grades of ranking before the black belt, comparable to the Japanese kyu. The lowest kup, that of a beginner, is eighth kup.

Kyudo 'Way of the bow'. Japanese martial art of archery with deep Zen concepts.

Lao Tzo or Tsu Legendary sage in Chinese history credited with founding Taoism. Author of the Chinese classic *The Tao Te Ching*.

Lo Han Name of any famous disciple of Buddha. A special series of exercises taught by Bodhidharma to the original monks at the Shaolin temple.

Marma-adi Secret teachings of striking the vital points in the Indian art of kalaripayit.

Martial art Pertaining to war arts, now means a fighting discipline to promote combat proficiency when unarmed or armed.

Mook Joong Wooden dummy, shaped like a man and used for conditioning and training purposes in many hard styles of kung fu.

Muay Thai Correct term for Thai boxing.

Naginata Japanese martial art, adopted mainly by women. Uses a spear with a curved blade about 3 feet long. In the modern combat sport form bamboo replaces the spear tip.

Naha Te One of the three original styles of Okinawan karate.

Ninja Secret society of mercenary assassins in Japan. It means 'stealers-in'. Trained from birth to become experts in death by assassination.

Ninjutsu Art or techniques of the ninja.

Nunchaku Two wooden batons linked by a short chain or cord to make an awesome weapon. Used originally as a rice flail in many parts of Southeast Asia.

Pa-Kua Internal style of kung fu, based on circular movements with open-palm hand strikes. It means 'eight trigrams' and the concept comes from the Chinese classic the *I Ching*, or book of changes.

Pentjak-Silat Indonesian martial art descended from Malaysian bersilat.

Praying Mantis Known in China as *tong long*. Named after Wong Long who invented the style after witnessing a fight between a grasshopper and a praying mantis.

Randori In judo, free practice or sparring where techniques are not prearranged.

Rokushakubo Okinawan 6 foot staff or pole made from oak or similar hardwood. *Roku* means 'six', *shaku* is about a foot length, *bo* means 'pole' or 'staff'.

Roundhouse Kick Kick used in virtually all martial arts. Its circular path gives it extra power from centrifugal force. It is probably one of the most powerful kicks in the martial artist's arsenal.

Ryu In Japanese martial arts, means 'school' or 'style'.

Sai Three-pronged forklike weapon once made of iron, now made of steel. Used mainly in karate for demonstration purposes. Resembles a very short blunt sword.

Samurai Japanese feudal warrior. The

word means 'one who serves'. Likened to the medieval knights of Europe. A Samurai served as a military retainer to the Daimyos and the Shogun. Samurai replaced the old word *bushi*, which means 'warrior'.

Savate Or *la savate*, French system of boxing and kicking related to Burmese bando and Thai boxing.

Sensei Japanese word for 'instructor' or 'teacher'.

Shaolin Temple in Hunan in China where allegedly kung fu was born.

Shinai Bamboo sword made of four strips bound together. Used in Kendo.

Shinobi Old term from which the word ninja was derived.

Shorinji Kempo Japanese karate with very strong Chinese kung fu influences, founded by its now deceased headmaster Doshin So. The organization in Japan is now headed by his daughter.

Shotokan School of Japanese karate founded by Gichin Funkoshi in 1922. Probably the most widely practiced style of karate in the world today.

Shuriken Throwing stars originally made of iron, sharply pointed and used by the ninja.

Sifu Instructor in kung fu; the word means 'father'.

Sil Lum Cantonese name for Shaolin.

Sport Karate Karate competition where contestants fight under combat rules in a ring or area. They wear protective gloves and foot pads. Techniques are scored and points are given. Actual contact is prohibited, although some leeway is allowed.

Sumo Ancient Japanese art of wrestling, steeped in quasi-religious aspects Contestants build themselves up to great weights in order to gain an advantage.

Taekwon-do Or *taekwondo*, Korean style of empty hand combat very similar to Japanese karate. As in karate-do, great emphasis is placed on strikes with hands and feet.

Tae Kyon Ancient Korean weaponless fighting art from which taekwon-do is said to be derived. Tae kyon officially became taekwon-do in 1945.

Tai-Chi Chuan Or *tai-chi* as it is more commonly known, one of the three major internal or soft arts of kung fu. Today more emphasis is placed on its therapeutic value to relieve stress and guide one into a state of tranquility. The word means 'great or grand ultimate fist'.

Tamashiwari Japanese technique of using strikes with the body against materials such as wood, tiles, bricks, ice, etc, to test the power or force of a strike.

Tang Shou Do Korean term, an alternative name for Chinese boxing.

Tang Soo Do 'Way of the tang hand'. Korean martial system similar to shotokan karate. Developed by Hwang Kee in 1949. Based on ancient Korean arts of t'ang su and subak.

Tao Chinese term meaning 'path' or 'way'. Tao is an invisible force or energy present in all things in the universe.

Te Japanese term meaning 'hand'.

Thai Boxing *See* MUAY THAI.

Thaing General term for Burmese arts of self-defense.

Tobok Suit worn to practice taekwon-do, consisting of a loose shirt and pants tied with a sash or belt.

Tonfa Okinawan weapon, once the handle used to operate a manual millstone. Used in karate to improve technique. Also a similar device used

in many US states as a police weapon to replace the now obsolete night stick or billy club.

White Belt In Japanese martial arts, color of a beginner.

Wing Chun Kung fu system invented by a woman. System studied by the late Bruce Lee on which to base his own system of jeet kune-do. Based on the law of economy of movement.

Wu Shu Generic term for the martial arts of mainland China.

Yang In Chinese cosmology, the positive aspect of the universe. Yang relates to male and light, one half of the Taoist view of the universe; characterized by positive action.

Yari Japanese weapon, a straight spear about 8 ft long. It replaced the naginata as a battlefield weapon. So far as is known, the yari never evolved as a sporting 'do' form.

Yin In chinese cosmology, the negative aspect of the universe. Relates to emptiness, softness, darkness, and female. Yin is the black fish with the white eye in the famous Yin-Yang symbol.

Yudansha Kendoka who has achieved the rank of black belt or higher. Only those of yudansha rank are permitted to wear an outfit that is of uniform color.

Zen Religious philosophy that claims that one can reach *satori*, or enlightenment, through meditation. Founded by the Indian monk Bodhidharma. Zen makes use of illogical poems called *koans* to clear the mind of trivia and so reach the meditative state required. In China Zen is called *Chan*. Zen was much favored by the Japanese Samurai.

789

PICTURE CREDITS